THE SUSTAINABLE DEVELOPMENT GOALS

T0309284

In 2015, the United Nations launched the Sustainable Development Goals (SDGs) to define and coordinate global priorities and aspirations up to 2030 in response to the economic, social and environmental challenges faced by the planet. Many governments across the world signed up for these goals. United Nations Secretary-General Ban Ki-Moon noted at the outset that business would be a vital partner in achieving the SDGs. This easy-to-digest book provides a critical evaluation of how a range of multinational companies from across different commercial sectors are currently addressing the SDGs and the challenges they are facing in contributing to them.

The private sector has thus been set the challenge of responding positively in support of the SDGs whilst at the same time acting in the shorter-term interests of its stakeholders. Using a wealth of illustrative materials drawn from company reports and other sources, this book looks at the response of 80 companies and organisations from eight different industry sectors. It examines the different approaches taken, discusses how far the SDGs are actively supported and reviews how progress is being assessed against related targets and objectives. In addition to an analysis of each industry sector, the book provides a summary overview of all industry sectors studied, identifying the most and least supported SDGs overall.

This book will be of interest to the fast-growing body of academics studying and researching sustainability, as well as to industry managers and public-sector operators involved in sustainability management and reporting. It provides detailed commentary and insights and identifies both key themes from the research and critical issues for the successful implementation of the SDGs in the period up to 2030.

Martin Wynn is Reader in Business Information Systems in the School of Business and Technology, University of Gloucestershire, and has written several books on technology transfer, planning and urban growth.

Peter Jones is Emeritus Professor in the School of Business and Technology, University of Gloucestershire.

THE SUSTAINABLE DEVELOPMENT GOALS

Industry Sector Approaches

Martin Wynn and Peter Jones

Routledge
Taylor & Francis Group

LONDON AND NEW YORK

First published 2020
by Routledge
2 Park Square, Milton Park, Abingdon, Oxon OX14 4RN

and by Routledge
52 Vanderbilt Avenue, New York, NY 10017

Routledge is an imprint of the Taylor & Francis Group, an informa business

British Library Cataloguing-in-Publication Data
A catalogue record for this book is available from the British Library

Library of Congress Cataloging-in-Publication Data
A catalog record for this book has been requested

ISBN: 978-0-367-23719-6 (hbk)
ISBN: 978-0-367-41880-9 (pbk)
ISBN: 978-0-429-28134-1 (ebk)

Typeset in Bembo
by Apex CoVantage, LLC

CONTENTS

FIGURES

TABLES

FOREWORD

In 2015, the United Nations (UN) launched the Sustainable Development Goals (SDGs) and associated targets. They did so in an effort to define and coordinate global priorities and aspirations up to 2030, noting a pressing need to address the economic, social and environmental challenges faced by the planet as a whole and to put the world on a sustainable path. Many governments across the world signed up for these goals.

But the private sector has also been called upon to play a leading role in their support and realisation. In the same year, UN Secretary-General Ban Ki-Moon noted that business would be a vital partner in achieving the SDGs and requested that all companies assess their environmental impact, set ambitious goals and communicate the results transparently. The UN agreement expressed a consensus by all governments that the SDGs would only be achieved with involvement of the private sector working alongside governments, parliaments, the UN system and other international institutions, local authorities, civil society, scientific and academic communities and people of all nations.

The private sector has thus been set the challenge of responding positively in support of the SDGs, whilst at the same time acting in the shorter-term interests of its stakeholders. Using a wealth of illustrative materials drawn from company reports and other sources, this book looks at the response of 80 companies and organisations from eight different industry sectors, including pharmaceuticals, financial services, information technology, marketing and media and energy, as well as the automobile industry and hotel and retail sectors. It assesses a wide range of approaches taken, discusses how far SDGs are actively supported and reviews how progress is being assessed against related targets and objectives. In addition to an analysis of each industry sector, the book provides a summary overview of all industry sectors studied, identifying the most and least supported SDGs overall.

This highly informative reference book will be of interest to the fast-growing body of academics studying and researching sustainability, as well as to industry managers and public-sector operators involved in sustainability management and reporting. It provides careful commentary and insights into different approaches and responses to the SDGs across a range of industry sectors. In concluding, it discusses both key themes from the research and critical issues for the successful implementation of the SDGs in the immediate future.

Jesse Norman, MP

ACKNOWLEDGEMENTS

Thanks are given to Daphne Comfort, formerly research administrator at the University of Gloucestershire, for her help in seeking out some of the material used in the book.

A number of companies and organisations have kindly agreed to the publication of figures and diagrams taken from their company reports and other sources. Grateful acknowledgement is thus given to the following:

Allianz SE
BP PLC
Credit Suisse
Deloitte LLP
Fiat Chrysler Automobiles Group
Fujitsu Technology Solutions
Hikma
InterContinental Hotels Group
International Tourism Partnership
John Lewis & Partners
PetroChina
Society of Motor Manufacturers and Traders
Tesco PLC
Virgin Media
Vodafone

INTRODUCTION

The Sustainable Development Goals (SDGs), agreed to at a UN General Assembly in 2015, embrace an ambitious and wide-ranging set of global environmental, social and economic issues; they were designed to effect a transition to a more sustainable future. The launch of the SDGs was intended to provide some consensus and common sense of purpose to sustainable development across the globe. The UN called on all governments to pursue these ambitious goals but also acknowledged the important role of the business community in addressing the SDGs. This introduction sketches out the characteristics and origins of the concept of sustainable development, outlines the development of the SDGs and explores how the case has been made to encourage business engagement with these ambitious goals. It also discusses the research methodology adopted in this study and the layout of the book.

Sustainable development origins and evolution

The terms "sustainable development," "sustainable" and "sustainability" have become increasingly widely used across many walks of life in recent decades. The ideas underpinning the concept of sustainable development are not new. Grober (2012), for example, claimed, "The idea of sustainability is not a mere mind game played by modern technocrats, nor the brainwave of some tree-hugging eco-warriors . . . it is our primal world cultural heritage" (p. 13). More specifically, Du Pisani (2006) provides a succinct summary of the historical roots and evolution of the concept of sustainability and looks to demonstrate "how the idea of sustainability evolved through the centuries as a counter to notions of progress" (p. 83). Du Pisani (2006) concludes by arguing

> that the roots of the concept of sustainability can be traced back to ancient times, but that population growth increases in consumption after the

Industrial Revolution, and the danger that crucial resources such as wood, coal and oil could be depleted boosted awareness of the need to use resources in a sustainable way. Fears that present and future generations might not be able to maintain their living standards stimulated a mode of thinking that would inform discourses which prepared the way for the emergence and global adoption of sustainable development.

(p. 87)

In the wake of the publication of the World Conservation Strategy (International Union for Conservation of Nature and Natural Resources, 1980) and Our Common Future (World Commission on Environment and Development, 1987), the concept of sustainable development began to attract increasing attention from the 1980s onwards. This increasing interest in sustainable development reflected growing concerns about a range of major challenges and problems facing societies, environments and economies on a variety of spatial and temporal scales. These concerns include continuing population growth and urbanisation and the pressures this is putting on natural resource consumption and food supplies, climate change, growing levels of pollution, loss of natural habitats, and water stress and the increasing scarcity of water resources in some areas of the world. In theory, the concept of sustainability has become increasingly seen as offering a potential solution to these problems. It is against this background that the SDGs were agreed to by the UN's member states in 2015 to establish the priorities for sustainable development through to 2030 (Table 0.1).

The most widely used definition of sustainable development is that provided by the World Commission on Environment and Development (1987) – namely, "development that meets the needs of the present without compromising the ability of future generations to meet their own needs" (p. 12). However, defining sustainable development is not straightforward, and there are a number of contrasting and contested meanings. There is a family of definitions essentially based in and around ecological principles, which focus on conserving natural resources and protecting fragile ecosystems on which ultimately all human life depends. Goodland (1995) defined environmental sustainability as "the maintenance of natural capital," arguing that it "seeks to improve human welfare by preserving the sources of raw materials used for human needs and ensuring that the sinks for human waste are not exceeded in order to prevent harm to humans" (p. 3).

There are also broader definitions that include social and economic dimensions, along with environmental and ecological goals and human needs to meet in an equitable manner. For the US Environment Protection Agency (2014), "sustainability creates and maintains the conditions under which humans and nature can exist in productive harmony, that permits fulfilling the social, economic and other requirements of present and future generations" (para.1).

Barr (2008) has claimed that "one of the most pressing and complex questions of the early twentieth-first century" is "how to promote the behavioural shifts necessary for creating the sustainable society" (p. xi). Diesendorf (2000) argued

TABLE 0.1 The SDGs

No.	Goal
1	End **poverty** in all its forms everywhere
2	End **hunger**, achieve food security and improved nutrition and promote sustainable agriculture
3	Ensure healthy lives and promote **well-being** or all at all ages
4	Ensure inclusive and equitable quality **education** and promote lifelong learning opportunities for all
5	Achieve **gender equality** and empower all women and girls
6	Ensure availability and sustainable management of **water and sanitation** for all
7	Ensure access to affordable, reliable, sustainable and modern **energy** for all
8	Promote sustained, inclusive and sustainable **economic growth**, full and productive **employment** and decent work for all
9	Build resilient **infrastructure**, promote inclusive and sustainable industrialisation and foster innovation
10	Reduce **inequality** within and amongst countries
11	Make **cities and human settlements** inclusive, safe, resilient and sustainable
12	Ensure sustainable **consumption and production** patterns
13	Take urgent action to combat **climate change** and its impacts
14	Conserve and sustainably use the **oceans, seas and marine resources** for sustainable development
15	Protect, restore and promote sustainable use of **terrestrial ecosystems**, sustainably manage forests, combat desertification, and halt and reverse land degradation and halt biodiversity loss
16	Promote **peaceful and inclusive societies** for sustainable development, provide access to justice for all and build effective, accountable and inclusive institutions at all levels
17	Strengthen the means of implementation and revitalise the **global partnership** for sustainable development

Source: Based on Deloitte, 2015, p. 2.

Note: Except when quoting other works, the SDGs are referred to in the text by their numbers only.

that sustainability can be seen as "the goals or endpoint of a process called sustainable development" (p. 3). More fundamentally, a distinction is often made between "weak" and "strong" sustainability, and Roper (2012) suggests that "weak sustainability prioritizes economic development, while strong sustainability subordinates economies to the natural environment and society, acknowledging ecological limits to growth" (p. 72). Sustainable development has proved a compelling but an elusive paradox (Adelson, Engell, Ranalli, & Van Anglen, 2008). Ramirez (2012), for example, has argued that this paradox reflects the tension between the potentially positive effects of economic growth on poverty and employment with the damaging impact of such growth on the environment's natural resources and on traditional societies and ways of life in many parts of the less developed world. More critically, Hudson (2005) argued that definitions of sustainable development range from "pallid blue green to dark deep green." He suggests the former centre on "technological fixes within current relations of production, essentially trading off economic against environmental objectives, with the market as the prime resource allocation mechanism," while for the latter, "prioritizing the preservation of nature is pre-eminent." He also notes that the dominant view of sustainable development "is grounded in a blue-green discourse of ecological modernization" and "claims that capital accumulation, profitable production and ecological sustainability are compatible goals." He further contrasts this view with the "deep green" perspective, which "would require significant reductions in living standards and radical changes in the dominant social relations of production" (p. 241).

While sustainable development has attracted widespread political support and has become applied in many areas of human endeavour, the concept has also attracted considerable criticism. For some commentators, sustainable development attracts hypocrites who use the language of sustainability to promote and defend unsustainable activities. A number of critics see the business interest in sustainable development, for example, as little more than a thinly veiled and cynical ploy, popularly described as "greenwash," designed to attract socially and environmentally conscious consumers while effectively sweeping pressing environmental and social concerns under the carpet. So seen, corporate commitments to sustainability might be characterised by what Hamilton (2009) described as "shifting consciousness towards what is best described as green consumerism" (pp. 573–574). Hamilton viewed this as "an approach that threatens to entrench the very attitudes and behaviors that are antithetical to sustainability" and argued "green consumerism has failed to induce significant inroads into the unsustainable nature of consumption and production" (p. 574). At the same time, there are concerns that the within the current capitalist global business model, the dominant view of sustainable development is delusional in that it fails to recognise that the current rates of economic growth are simply unsustainable. As such it draws attention away, not only from the need to develop new ways of organising how people can relate to the natural world but also from the need for fundamental and widespread social and political change. Indeed, Mansfield (2009) has argued, "It is striking the extent to which politics – relations of power – have been written out of the discussions about sustainability" (p. 37).

The SDGs

The SDGs (Table 0.1) came into effect in January 2016, and they will guide UN development thinking and policy up to 2030. The United Nations (2015a) described the SDGs as the UN "2030 Agenda for Sustainable Development," "a plan of action for people, planet and prosperity," which is designed to "shift the world on to a sustainable and resilient path" (para.1). The European Commission (2017) argued,

> The scale, ambition and approach of the Agenda are unprecedented. One key feature is that the SDGs are global in nature and universally applicable, taking into account national realities, capacities and levels of development and

specific challenges. All countries have a shared responsibility to achieve the SDGs, and all have a meaningful role to play locally, nationally as well as on the global scale.

(para.5)

Further, the European Commission (2017) argued, "The 2030 Agenda integrates in a balanced manner the three dimensions of sustainable development – economic, social and environmental" and that it is "indivisible, in a sense that it must be implemented as a whole, in an integrated rather than a fragmented manner, recognizing that the different goals and targets are closely interlinked" (para.6).

The 17 SDGs encompass a wide range of global challenges, from "the wellbeing of every individual to the health of the planet, from infrastructure to institutions, from governance to green energy, peaceful societies to productive employment" (Institute of Human Rights and Business, 2015, p. 12), with each one having a number of associated targets. The ratification of the SDGs is the latest in the line of global sustainable development initiatives, which can be traced back to the declaration designed "to inspire and guide the peoples of the world in the preservation and enhancement of the human environment" (United Nations Environment Programme, 1972, p. 1), following the UN Conference on the Human Environment held in Stockholm in 1971. The SDGs are seen to build on the UN's Millennium Development Goals (MDGs) established in 2001. The MDGs were described as having "produced the most successful anti-poverty movement in history" (United Nations, 2015b, p. 3), but other assessments of the achievements of the MDGs have been less positive. While Fehling, Nelson and Venkatapuram (2013), for example, acknowledged that "remarkable progress has been made," they argued that "progress across all MDGs has been limited and uneven across countries" (p. 1109). At the same time, the involvement of the business community in the MDGs was limited with PricewaterhouseCoopers (2015) commenting, "Business, for the most part, didn't focus on the MDGs because they were aimed at developing countries." They added, however, that with the advent of the SDGs "sustainability is moving from the corporate sidelines into the mainstream" (p. 6).

Apart from the SDGs themselves, there are 169 associated targets in what the Institute of Human Rights and Business (2015) described as "a genuinely comprehensive vision of the future" in which "little is left unaddressed" from "the wellbeing of every individual to the health of the planet, from infrastructure to institutions, from governance to green energy, peaceful societies to productive employment" (p. 12). As examples, the targets for 2030 for SDG1 include eradicating extreme poverty, measured as people living on $1.25 per day, ensuring that all men and women and particularly the poor and vulnerable have equal rights to economic resources, access to basic services and ownership and control over land and property, as well as building the resilience of the poor and vulnerable to reduce their exposure to climate change–related extreme events (Table 0.2). For SDG6, the 2030 targets include achieving universal and equitable access to safe and affordable drinking water for all: protecting and restoring water related ecosystems and

TABLE 0.2 Targets for SDG1: end poverty in all its forms, everywhere

1.1	By 2030, eradicate extreme poverty for all people everywhere, currently measured as people living on less than $1.25 a day.
1.2	By 2030, reduce at least by half the proportion of men, women and children of all ages living in poverty in all its dimensions according to national definitions.
1.3	Implement nationally appropriate social protection systems and measures for all, including floors, and by 2030 achieve substantial coverage of the poor and the vulnerable.
1.4	By 2030, ensure that all men and women, in particular the poor and the vulnerable, have equal rights to economic resources, as well as access to basic services, ownership and control over land and other forms of property, inheritance, natural resources, appropriate new technology and financial services, including microfinance.
1.5	By 2030, build the resilience of the poor and those in vulnerable situations and reduce their exposure and vulnerability to climate-related extreme events and other economic, social and environmental shocks and disasters.
1.a	Ensure significant mobilisation of resources from a variety of sources, including through enhanced development cooperation, in order to provide adequate and predictable means for developing countries, in particular least developed countries, to implement programmes and policies to end poverty in all its dimensions.
1.b	Create sound policy frameworks at the national, regional and international levels, based on pro-poor and gender-sensitive development strategies, to support accelerated investment in poverty eradication actions.

Source: Based on United Nations, 2017.

improving water quality by reducing pollution, eliminating dumping and minimising the release of hazardous chemicals.

Targets for SDG12 include achieving the sustainable management and efficient use of natural resources by 2030, halving per capital global food waste at the retail and consumer levels, reducing food losses along production and supply chains by 2030 and designing and implementing tools to monitor sustainable development impacts for sustainable tourism that creates jobs and promotes local culture and products. In addition, for every target, there are one or more "indicators," there being 241 in all (United Nations, 2017). For example, for target 3.1, which is "by 2030, reduce the global maternal mortality ratio to less than 70 per 100,000 live births," the indicators are the "maternal mortality ratio" (3.1.1) and the "proportion of births attended by skilled health personnel" (3.1.2). Table 0.3 shows the indicators for targets 13.1 and 13.2.

In some ways, SDG17, which recognises that the SDGs can only be realised with a strong commitment to partnership and cooperation, is an overarching goal, which binds all the other goals together. MDG Monitor (2016) argued,

> If the reference to accountability and monitoring of data is taken seriously in SDG17, this aspect could help in unlocking the full potential of all the SDGs to be a great influence for good. Creating people-centred strategies for

TABLE 0.3 Example of SDG indicators: for SDG13 targets 13.1 and 13.2

Target	Indicator
13.1 Strengthen resilience and adaptive capacity to climate-related hazards and natural disasters in all countries	13.1.1 Number of deaths, missing persons and directly affected persons attributed to disasters per 100,000 population 13.1.2 Number of countries that adopt and implement national disaster risk reduction strategies in line with the Sendai Framework for Disaster Risk Reduction 2015–2030 13.1.3 Proportion of local governments that adopt and implement local disaster risk reduction strategies in line with national disaster risk reduction strategies
13.2 Integrate climate change measures into national policies, strategies and planning	13.2.1 Number of countries that have communicated the establishment or operationalisation of an integrated policy/strategy/plan, which increases their ability to adapt to the adverse impacts of climate change and foster climate resilience and low greenhouse gas emissions development in a manner that does not threaten food production (including a national adaptation plan, nationally determined contribution, national communication, biennial update report or other)

Source: Based on United Nations, 2017.

> gathering data, accompanied by strong citizen performance monitoring will be crucial to holding decision makers accountable.
>
> *(para. 10)*

However, MDG Monitor (2016) also counselled caution in that

> fostering the gathering of citizen-generated, independent data will need the implementation of certain key conditions. These conditions include respecting the basic freedoms of association, peaceful assembly and expression. So far, the situation is not good as CIVICUS reported that in 2014, 96 countries violated these rights substantially.
>
> *(para. 11)*

The importance of SDG17 is reflected in the targets it spans, which include finance, technology, trade, capacity building and systemic issues, as well as the role of the private sector.

The role of businesses in addressing the SDGs

The Institute of Human Rights and Business (2015) noted that, for the achievement of the SDGs,

> the private sector has been highlighted as a partner with the potential to contribute in multiple ways to development objectives: by stimulating economic

growth and job creation, providing investment and finance and sharing the resources and knowledge needed to shape innovative solutions to global challenges.

(p. 5)

As investors, consumers, governments, interest groups and the media have become more acutely aware of the environmental, social and economic impacts of business activities, so too have corporate sustainability initiatives assumed ever-increasing importance.

Stuart Gulliver, group chief executive of HSBC Holdings plc, has commented,

> The Sustainable Development Goals provide a focus for the world's efforts to meet global challenges including climate change, water management and sanitation and equitable education. The opportunity clearly exists for the private sector to create and commercialise sustainable solutions at scale.
>
> *(United Nations Global Compact and KPMG, 2016, p. 15)*

In many ways, the launch of the SDGs was designed to provide a broad consensus and common sense of purpose to sustainable development across the globe. The UN and KPMG note

> the agreement on a new sustainable development agenda expresses a consensus by all Governments that the SDGs can only be achieved with involvement of the private sector working alongside Governments, Parliaments, the UN system and other international institutions, local authorities, civil society, the scientific and academic community – and all people.

They add that governments in the post-2015 era "call on all businesses to apply their creativity and innovation to solving sustainable development challenges" (United Nations Global Compact and KPMG, 2016, p. 2). Thus, while national governments clearly have a vital role to play in addressing the SDGs, the role of private-sector engagement with the SDGs may provide the ultimate testing ground for their successful implementation. PricewaterhouseCoopers (2015), however, sounded a word of caution for how companies will help deliver the SDGs:

> It's not about tweaking what they do, but looking at core strategy. With no holistic view or understanding of how the SDGs interlink with each other, or if a positive impact in one area creates a negative impact in another, it may prove complex to navigate . . . there will not be a "one size fits all" answer.
>
> (p. 4)

More specifically, the Global Reporting Initiative/United Nations Global Compact/World Business Council for Sustainable Development (2015) suggested that that companies that look to employ the SDGs as a framework to shape and report their strategies would be able to realise a number of benefits. For example, sustainable development challenges are presenting market opportunities for companies to develop innovative energy efficient technologies, to reduce greenhouse gas emissions and waste and to meet the needs of largely untapped markets for healthcare, education, finance and communication products and services in less developed economies. By enhancing the value of corporate sustainability and, more specifically, by integrating sustainability across the value chain, it is argued that companies can protect and create value for themselves by increasing sales, developing new markets, strengthening its brands, improving operational efficiency and enhancing employee loyalty and reducing staff turnover. It is suggested that companies that work to advance the SDGs will improve trust amongst their stakeholders, reduce regulatory and legal risks and build resilience to future cost increases and regulatory and legislative requirements. Companies should look to adopt a strategic approach in assessing their current and possible future impacts on the SDGs with the focus being on looking to enhance positive impacts and to reduce negative impacts. In making such an assessment, companies should look to map the SDGs against their value chain and to engage with both internal and external stakeholders and particularly to give due attention to future impacts on the environment and to disadvantaged and marginalised groups. At the same time, it is argued that companies must look to integrate sustainability into their core business across the whole of the supply chain.

Related theory and research methodology

As interest in sustainable development has gathered momentum, so a number of attempts have been made to develop theoretical frameworks connecting nature and society. Todorov and Marinova (2009), for example, reviewed the models being developed to conceptualise what they describe as "an extremely complex concept" (p. 1217), and they presented a fivefold classification for sustainability — models – namely, quantitative models, physical models, standardising models, conceptual models and pictorial visualisation models. The first two of these model types tend to be restricted to specific disciplines; the third is concerned with the development and application of sustainability indicators, while the final two seek to link the environmental, social and economic dimensions of sustainability. They acknowledge that the conceptual category of models is very broad, and they trace its origins from the work of the Club of Rome formed in the late 1960s and limits to growth (Meadows, Meadows, Randers, & Behrens, 1972), through to much more recent work on climate change (Intergovernmental Panel on Climate Change, 2007). The pictorial visualisation models adopt a simple three-dimensional representation of sustainability with the three dimensions – namely, environmental, social and economic – being represented either as pillars or in a Venn diagram as three overlapping circles. While Todorov and Marinova (2009) suggest that such models are "static," they commend them as being "powerful in reaching a broad audience" (p. 1218).

A number of authors (e.g. Barter, 2011; Zink, 2005; Garvare & Johansson, 2010) have employed stakeholder theory to conceptualise sustainability. In simple terms, stakeholder theory is developed around the belief that companies should be sensitive to the interests not only of their shareholders but also those of a wider variety of stakeholders, including suppliers, customers and society at large, and that in so doing, they will ultimately be more successful. Wheeler, Colbert and Freeman (2003), for example, suggested that "sustainability is a construct whose foundational ideas are consonant with those of stakeholder theory" and that "stakeholder concepts are highly relevant and useful to thinking about sustainability" (p. 16). In developing a model of stakeholder management for sustainability, Garvare and Johansson (2010) argued that "contemporary organisations must satisfy a variety of stakeholders" (p. 737), and Steurer, Langer, Konrad and Martinuzzi (2005) explored the relationship between sustainability and stakeholder theory and examined how "corporations are confronted with economic, social and environmental stakeholder claims" (p. 264).

There have been attempts to develop a more critical theory, which embraces the different and competing perspectives outlined earlier. Amsler (2009), for example, has argued, "The contested politics and ambiguities of sustainability discourses" can be embraced to develop a "critical theory of sustainability" (p. 127). Amsler further argued that current debates should be located "within a broader tradition of social criticism" and that "competing interpretations of sustainability" should be viewed as "invitations to explore the complex processes through which competing visions of just futures are produced, resisted and realized" (p. 125). Castro (2004) sought to lay the foundations for a more radical theory of sustainability by questioning the very possibility of sustainable development under capitalism and arguing that economic growth relies upon the continuing and inevitable exploitation of both natural and social capital.

The research methodology is based on an extensive review of existing literature and industry reports. Each chapter draws its empirical material from annual and corporate sustainability reports published by the leading players in the respective industry sectors, from reports published by a number of industry and industry-related organisations and from academic papers. Further, the book adopts the approach recommended by Saidani, Yannon, Leroy and Cluzel (2017) in that while the inclusion of peer-reviewed academic papers "ensures scientific soundness," corporate and industry body reports can be seen to "reflect current industrial reality and needs . . . and therefore bring meaningful insights" (para.5). This study addresses the following research questions:

- How have different industry sectors responded to the challenges set by the SDGs?
- What are the key themes arising from the varying approaches to the SDGs adopted by different industry sectors?
- What are the critical issues for the future continued support and delivery of the SDGs?

The authors conducted a range of Internet searches in the period of January 2018 to July 2019, using Google as the search engine. First, a search was undertaken on Google using the names of leading companies in the industry sector, with the term "sustainability report" as the key words. The most recent report of these companies was then searched using terms relating to the SDGs. A second set of searches was then undertaken on Google using the terms "sustainability" and "SDGs", which produced a number of industry, organisation, and industry-related reports. All the corporate and industry reports identified in these two searches are in the public domain, and the authors took the considered view that they did not need to contact the selected companies or organisations to obtain formal permission prior to conducting their research. Third, a search was undertaken on Google Scholar using "sustainability and the SDGs" in the particular industry sector as the key words, and this produced a number of academic research papers. Finally, works referenced in these sources were pursued for further information.

Framework analysis (Mason, Mirza, & Webb, 2018) was used to identify and organise the key issues and concepts discussed in each chapter. This technique was originally developed by Ritchie and Spencer (1994) for the management of qualitative data in applied policy research and has been deployed for qualitative analysis in a number of areas, including research into the health (Gale, Health, Cameron, Rashid, & Redwood, 2013), psychological (Parkinson, Eatough, Holmes, Stapley, & Midgley, 2016) and sociological (Neale, 2012) fields. A matrix is set up consisting of the papers and reports reviewed along one axis and the broad categories and sub-categories relating to sustainability and the SDGs on the other. From here, the matrix is developed to comprise a range of cells containing different themes or topics. Each cell in the matrix contains summarised data organised by report and theme. This allows for large amounts of data to be readily viewed and compared by reading across reports and comparing and developing emergent themes.

Layout of the book

This book examines how companies from different industry sectors have approached the SDGs since their launch in 2015. It does not attempt to make generalisations about these sectors but rather provides examples from these sectors from which key issues are distilled and discussed. The book is organised into nine chapters. The first eight chapters examine the approach to the SDGs by eight different industry sectors, and Chapter 9 provides a cross-sector analysis and conclusion.

Each of the eight core chapters have a common structure. Following a brief introductory section, an overview of how the ten companies or organisations in the sector have addressed the SDGs is given. The following section then provides some detailed examples of how specific SDGs have been pursued and supported in different national and organisational contexts. There are many such examples from available reports and websites, and those selected here are intended as illustration only rather than as a comprehensive survey. Nevertheless, issues that emerge from these detailed examples, and from the more wide-ranging overview, are then discussed and summarised, and the final section of each chapter provides a brief overall conclusion.

The concluding chapter addresses the three research questions posed earlier. It examines the different approaches of industry sectors to the SDGs, discusses key themes emerging from cross-industry analysis and identifies key issues for the continued support and progression of the SDGs.

References

Adelson, G., Engell, J., Ranalli, B., & Van Anglen, K. (Eds.). (2008). *Environment: An interdisciplinary anthology*. Retrieved November 21, 2016, from www.environmentanthology.org/index.php/concepts-a-case-studies/ch-5-the-paradox-ofsustainable-development/295

Amsler, S. S. (2009). Embracing the politics of ambiguity: Towards a normative theory of sustainability. *Capitalism, Nature and Socialism, 20*(2), 111–125.

Barr, S. (2008). *Environment and society: Sustainability, policy and the citizen*. Aldershot: Ashgate.

Barter, M. (2011). *Stakeholder theory: Pictures, the environment and sustainable development -do we have enough pictures in our heads or do we need something different?* Asia Pacific Work in Progress Research Paper Series, No. 4. Retrieved November 3, 2014, from www.griffith.edu.au/data/assets/pdf_file/0009/378693/APWIPPs_Issue-4.pdf

Castro, C. (2004). Sustainable development: Mainstream and critical perspectives. *Organisation and Environment, 17*(2), 195–225.

Deloitte. (2015). *How Deloitte supports the United Nations sustainable development goals*. Retrieved March 23, 2019, from https://www2.deloitte.com/content/dam/Deloitte/global/Documents/About-Deloitte/gx_SDGs_Deloitte.pdf

Diesendorf, M. (2000). Sustainability and sustainable development. In D. Dunphy, J. Benveniste, A. Griffiths, & P. Sutton (Eds.), *Sustainability: The corporate challenge of the 21st century* (pp. 19–37). Sydney: Allen & Unwin.

Du Pisani, J. A. (2006). Sustainable development – historical roots of the concept. *Environmental Sciences, 3*(2), 83–96.

European Commission. (2017). *The 2010 agenda for sustainable development and the SDGs*. Retrieved June 10, 2019, from http://ec.europa.eu/environment/sustainable-development/SDGs/index_en.htm

Fehling, M., Nelson, B., & Venkatapuram, S. (2013). Limitations of the millennium development goals: A literature review. *Public Health, 8*(10), 1109–1122. Retrieved June 10, 2019, from www.ncbi.nlm.nih.gov/pmc/articles/PMC3877943/

Gale, N., Health, G., Cameron, E., Rashid, S., & Redwood, S. (2013). Using the framework method for the analysis of qualitative data in multi-disciplinary health research. *BMC Medical Research Methodology, 13*, 117.

Gavare, R., & Johansson, P. (2010). Management for sustainability: A stakeholder theory. *Total Quality Management, 21*(7), 737–744.

Global Reporting Initiative/United Nations Global Compact/World Business Council for Sustainable Development. (2015). *SDG compass: The guide for business action on the SDGs*. Retrieved June 10, 2019, from https://sdgcompass.org/wp-content/uploads/2015/12/019104_SDG_Compass_Guide_2015.pdf

Goodland, R. (1995). The concept of environmental sustainability. *Annual Review of Ecology and Systematics, 26*, 1–24.

Grober, U. (2012). *Sustainability: A cultural history* (R. Cunningham, Trans.). Cambridge: Green Books.

Hamilton, C. (2009). Consumerism, self-creation and prospects for a new ecological consciousness. *Journal of Cleaner Production, 18*(6), 571–575.

Hudson, R. (2005). Towards sustainable economic practices, flows and spaces: Or is the necessary impossible and the impossible necessary? *Sustainable Development, 13*(4), 239–252.

Institute for Human Rights and Business. (2015). *State of play- business and the sustainable development goals: Mind the gap – challenges for implementation*. Retrieved June 8, 2019, from www.ihrb. org/media/images/reports/state_of_play_report-business_and_the_sdgs.pdf

Intergovernmental Panel on Climate Change (2007). Climate Change 2007: Synthesis Report. Contribution of Working Groups I, II and III to the Fourth Assessment Report of the Intergovernmental Panel on Climate Change [Core Writing Team, Pachauri, R.K and Reisinger, A. (Eds.)]. IPCC, Geneva, Switzerland.

International Union for the Conservation of Nature and Natural Resources. (1980). *World conservation strategy*. Retrieved November 23, 2013, from https://portals.iucn.org/library/efiles/documents/WCS-004.pdf

Mansfield, B. (2009). Sustainability. In N. Castree, D. Demeriff, D. Liverman, & B. Rhoads (Eds.), *A companion to environmental geography* (pp. 37–49). London: Wiley.

Mason, W., Mirza, N., & Webb, C. (2018). Using the framework method to analyze mixed-methods case studies. In *Sage research methods cases* (Part 2). Retrieved October 7, 2019, from http://dx.doi.org/10.4135/9781526438683

MDG Monitor. (2016). *SDG 17 – Sustainable development through global partnerships*. Retrieved June 10, 2019, from www.mdgmonitor.org/sdg17-sustainable-development-through-global-partnerships/

Meadows, D., Meadows, D. L., Randers, J., & Behrens, W. (1972). *The limits to growth*. New York: Universe Books.

Neale, B. (2012). *Qualitative longitudinal research: An introduction to the timescapes methods guides series*. Timescapes Methods Guides Series, No. 1 [online]. Retrieved October 7, 2019, from http://followingfathers.leeds.ac.uk/findings-and-publications/

Parkinson, S., Eatough, V., Holmes, J., Stapley, E., & Midgley, N. (2016). Framework analysis: A worked example of a study exploring young people's experiences of depression. *Qualitative Research in Psychology, 13*(2), 109–129.

PricewaterhouseCoopers. (2015). *Making it your business: Engaging with the sustainable development goals*. Retrieved June 10, 2019, from www.pwc.com/gx/en/sustainability/SDG/SDG%20Research_FINAL.pdf

Ramirez, G. A. (2012). Sustainable development: Paradoxes, misunderstandings and learning organisations. *The Learning Organisation, 19*(1), 58–76.

Ritchie, J., & Spencer, L. (1994). Qualitative data analysis for applied policy research. In A. Bryman & R. Burgess (Eds.), *Analyzing qualitative data* (pp. 173–194). London: Taylor & Francis.

Roper, J. (2012). Environmental risk, sustainability discourses and public relations. *Public Relations Inquiry, 1*(1), 69–87.

Saidani, M., Yannon, B., Leroy, Y., & Cluzel, F. (2017). How to assess product performance in the circular economy? Proposed requirements for the design of a circularity measurement framework. *Recycling, 2*(1) [online]. Retrieved June 10, 2019, from www.mdpi.com/2313-4321/2/1/6/htm

Steurer, R., Langer, M., Konrad, A., & Martinuzzi, A. (2005). Corporations, stakeholders and sustainable development I: A theoretical exploration of business – society relations. *Journal of Business Ethics, 61*(3), 263–281.

Todorov, V. I., & Marinova, D. (2009). *Models of sustainability*. Presented at the World IMACS/MODSIM Congress, Cairns, Australia. Retrieved April 13, 2014, from www.mssanz.org.au/modsim09/D2/todorov_D2a.pdf

United Nations. (2015a). *Transforming our world: The 2030 agenda for sustainable development*. Retrieved June 8, 2019, from https://sustainabledevelopment.un.org/post2015/transformingourworld

United Nations. (2015b). *The millennium development goals report 2015.* Retrieved June 10, 2019, from www.un.org/millenniumgoals/2015_MDG_Report/pdf/MDG%202015%20rev% 20(July%201).pdf

United Nations. (2017). *Summary table of SDG indicators.* Retrieved June 8, 2019, from https://unstats.un.org/sdgs/files/meetings/iaeg-sdgs-meeting-06/Summary%20Table_ Global%20Indicator%20Framework_08.11.2017.pdf

United Nations Environment Programme. (1972). *Declaration of the United Nations conference on the human environment.* Retrieved June 10, 2019, from www.soas.ac.uk/cedep-demos/000_P514_IEL_K3736-Demo/treaties/media/1972%20Stockholm%20 1972%20-%20Declaration%20of%20the%20United%20Nations%20Conference%20 on%20the%20Human%20Environment%20-%20UNEP.pdf

United Nations Global Compact and KPMG. (2016). *SDG industry matrix – financial services.* Retrieved June 10, 2019, from https://sustainabledevelopment.un.org/content/ documents/9789CRT046599%20SDG_Financial%20Services_29sep_WEB-1.pdf

United States Environment Protection Agency. (2014). *Sustainability: What is sustainability?* Retrieved June 8, 2019, from www.epa.gov/sustainability/learn-about-sustainability#what

Wheeler, D., Colbert, B., & Freeman, R. E. (2003). Focusing on value: Reconciling corporate social responsibility, sustainability and a stakeholder approach in a network world. *Journal of General Management, 61*(3), 1–28.

World Commission on Environment and Development. (1987). *Our common future.* Retrieved June 9, 2019, from https://sustainabledevelopment.un.org/content/documents/5987our-common-future.pdf

Zink, K. J. (2005). Stakeholder orientation and corporate social responsibility as a precondition for sustainability. *Total Quality Management and Business Excellence, 16*(8–9), 1041–1052.

1

THE FINANCIAL SERVICES INDUSTRY

Introduction

While large international companies dominate the financial services industry, it also includes a diverse range of smaller companies. The larger companies are located in major financial centres, including London, New York, Hong Kong, Shanghai and Zurich. Weber, Diaz and Schwegler (2014) have noted "financial sector performance is relatively low regarding corporate social responsibility" (p. 321), which accords with Scholtens (2006) earlier stated view that "there appears to be much more scope for finance to promote socially and environmentally desirable activities and to discourage detrimental activities than has been acknowledged in the academic literature so far" (p. 19). More recently, other authors have emphasised the central role that the financial services sector can play in promoting the SDGs. One Stone Advisors (2017), the international sustainability consultants, for example, argued that "financial institutions are vital in achieving the UN SDGs" and suggested "fuelling the transition to a sustainable and inclusive global economy by 2030 will require vast amounts of capital, estimated at $507 trillion each year–with up to $93 trillion for climate change solutions alone." They concluded, "Most of this money must come from the private sector" and that "financial institutions therefore have a key role to play in redirecting mainstream funds to promote sustainable growth and improving access to financial services so no one is left behind" (p. 2). Similarly, Anjuli Pandit, primary sustainability manager at BNP Paribas Global Markets (BNP Paribas, 2019) notes,

> The financial services industry has a central role to play. Its power to influence who gets the money is critical. We have to find the money to create solutions to these problems – and move money away from places that are causing them.
>
> *(para. 12)*

At the international level, the United Nations Environment Programme (UNEP) Finance Initiative (2018) announced plans agreed to by 26 banks from across 5 continents to work together to "redefine how the banking industry delivers a more sustainable future" and "to align the sector with the UN SDGs and the Paris Climate Agreement" (para.3). Although these plans are undoubtedly ambitious, and it remains to be seen how the principles will be developed in practice, they would seem to represent a clear notice of intention by some of the world's major banks to address the SDGs. This chapter provides a review of how major financial services companies are responding to these challenges in addressing the SDGs. The companies included in this review are Citibank, the consumer division of international financial services company Citigroup, which has over 7,500 branches in some 20 countries; Barclays, a British multinational investment bank and financial services company, headquartered in London, with almost 80,000 employees operating in 50 countries; HSBC, a British multinational and one of the largest banking and financial services organisations in the world, with operations in 66 countries and territories; BNP Paribas, a French international banking group with both retail banking and investment banking operations, operating in 77 countries across five continents; Credit Suisse, a Swiss multinational investment bank and financial services company, based in Switzerland, with operations in 50 countries and over 46,000 employees; Standard Chartered, a British multinational banking and financial services company headquartered in London, employing 87,000 people in 70 countries; AXA, a French multinational insurance firm headquartered in Paris that engages in global insurance, investment management, and other financial services; Allianz, a German multinational financial services company headquartered in Munich, which was judged the world's largest insurance company and the largest financial services group in 2014 by *Forbes* magazine; Crédit Agricole, the world's largest cooperative financial institution, consisting of a network of Crédit Agricole local banks, the 39 Crédit Agricole regional banks and a central institute, the Crédit Agricole S.A; and Deloitte, the fourth-largest privately owned company in the United States, one of the "Big Four" accounting organisations and the largest professional services network in the world by revenue and number of professionals.

Overview of the financial services industry and the SDGs

There are marked variations in the extent to which the leading financial services companies have responded to the challenges posed by the SDGs (Table 1.1). While some companies report on how they are addressing specific SDGs, others seem to have been more reluctant to make public commitments to these challenges. The banks, for example, vary in the extent to which they publicly report on their commitment to the SDGs. Barclays (2019), whilst expressing support for all the SDGs, noted that "Goal 8 – Decent Work and Economic Growth – is an area where Barclays can have substantial, first-hand impact" (para.3). To address this, Barclays CEO Jeff Staley highlighted Barclays's "commitment is to upskill millions of people and help drive job creation." He also maintained that the company was

> helping people gain access to the vital skills they need to get into work. By addressing the challenges people have in finding employment, we believe that the individual's social and economic prospects increase, which in turn creates broader opportunities for growth and helps build long-term demand for banking services.
>
> *(para. 4)*

In 2017, HSBC launched a new style of corporate sustainable bond based on the UN SDGs. HSBC intended to use the proceeds of the bond to partly, or wholly, finance businesses and projects that promote certain SDGs selected by HSBC. In launching this bond, HSBC (2017) recognised "we have responsibilities not only towards our customers, employees and shareholders, but also to the countries and communities in which we operate" (p. 2). The company also reported "as part of our legacy as a strong corporate citizen, HSBC recognises the catalysing role it can play through its lending activities and operations towards the achievement of the SDGs" (p. 2). HSBC committed itself to providing an annual progress report, which will include both allocation and impact reporting. The allocation report will focus on the aggregate amounts of funds allocated to each of the SDGs and a description of the types of businesses and projects financed, while the impact report will provide quantitative details, HSBC also commissioned an external assurance process to review its annual progress reports and reported that both the progress report and the external assurance statement would be available to the public via the Internet. In April 2019, HSBC (2019) issued "Environmental, Social and Governance Update," in which they identified SDGs 4, 7, 8, 11, 12 and 13 as being "in close alignment to our strategy" and "we will contribute to these through our financing and investments, as well as how we conduct business and operate" (p. 35).

In their latest corporate social responsibility (CSR) report, BNP Paribas (2019) notes that "the Sustainable Development Goals aim to end poverty by 2030 while protecting our planet's environment. As a global company and bank, BNP Paribas has a key role to play in this collective effort" (para.1). The company claim to "have mapped our entire business to the UN's SDGs." In the context of SDG12 and SDG13, the company claims "we are leaders in green bonds and are developing other products like positive incentive loans, which give corporates reduced rates if they exceed their sustainability targets, or charge more if they fall short" (BNP Paribas, 2018, para.8). In addition, "we have made decisions on our loan book to support the energy transition" and "have divested from areas we don't believe will be productive in the future – such as new coal-fired power plants – and we have an active target of £15billion investment in renewable energy" (para.7). In addition, as regards their own company performance, "we have set science-based targets for ourselves to reduce our carbon footprint towards the 1.5C scenario – the globally agreed level at which to limit temperature rise to curb global warming" (para.7).

TABLE 1.1 SDGs addressed by financial services companies

SDG/ financial company	HSBC	Standard Chartered	Citibank	Credit Suisse	AXA	Deloitte	Allianz	Barclays	BNP Paribas	Credit Agricole
1		x			x	x	x	x		x
2						x		x		x
3		x			x	x		x	x	x
4	x	x		x		x		x		x
5		x	x	x	x	x		x		x
6		x				x		x		x
7	x	x	x	x		x	x	x		x
8	x	x	x	x		x	x	x		x
9		x	x	x	x	x		x		x
10		x				x		x	x	x
11	x	x	x	x	x	x		x		x
12	x	x				x		x	x	x
13	x	x	x	x	x	x	x	x	x	x
14						x		x		x
15				x		x		x		x
16		x				x		x		
17		x	x			x		x		

Citibank (2017) claimed, "As a global bank Citi believes it is important for us to take a leading role in contributing to the UN's SDGs." Further, Citibank (2017) "identified seven goals on which we can have the greatest impact" (p. 2) – namely, SDGs 5, 7, 8, 9, 11, 13 and 17. The bank maintains that "the SDGs underscore a continuation of the work we've been doing for more than 200 years: innovating financing solutions to help clients meet the world's toughest challenges." They also note "through our core business, we have already helped to mobilize billions from the capital markets to support environmental and social progress, areas we have been publicly reporting on since 2000," though the company reported "while we do not underestimate the challenge, we look forward to embracing it head on to do our part in contributing to this important global goal" (p. 7).

Investment bank Credit Suisse (2015) claimed, "As a global bank, identifying and responding to client demand and working with clients and partner organizations, Credit Suisse can contribute to a wide range of SDGs in a variety of ways" (p. 11). Some of the bank's early endeavours have focussed on

> raising awareness of the SDGs, of discussing the role and responsibility of the banking sector, and of identifying priorities for action as well as opportunities

to organize and build partnerships to attain the SDGs. A key finding expressed by most participants was that banks are expected to embed the consideration of environmental and social matters into core financial products and services and to put greater emphasis on the development of innovative investment solutions.

(Credit Suisse, 2018, para.2)

More specifically, Credit Suisse have targeted SDGs 4, 5, 7, 8, 9, 11, 13 and 15 (Credit Suisse, 2019, p. 59). The bank argued, for example, that

by applying our expertise to capital market transactions and investment solutions to develop renewable energy technologies, we contribute to SDG7, sustainable energy, and by increasing energy efficiency in our operational premises and our real estate investment portfolio, we address SDG9, resilient infrastructure, and SDG11, sustainable cities.

(Credit Suisse, 2018, para.5)

Standard Chartered Bank (2019) reported, "Our sustainability aspirations build on our three sustainability pillars with measurable targets to demonstrate how we are achieving sustainable outcomes across our business" and that "these also allow us to measure our contribution to the United Nations Sustainable Development Goals" (p. 1). The company's three pillars are "contributing to sustainable economic growth," "being a responsible company" and "investing in communities." For each of these, there is a range of aspirations linked to the SDGs with specific targets. For pillar three (investing in communities), community engagement is the main aspiration, being linked to SDGs 3, 4, 5, 10 and 17. The targets include, for example, as regards entrepreneurship, to "reach 50,000 micro and small businesses" between January 2019 and December 2023. The company links these aspirations in some regards to SDGs 1, 3–13, 16 and 17.

Within the insurance sector, AXA (2017) claimed that "through its activities, investments and strategic focus," the company "is a responsible actor and attentive to its environment" and that all its "responsible actions are aligned with the UN SDGs" (p. 46). At the same time, the company claimed, "The value created by AXA cannot be measured simply in financial terms. Our approach to the insurance business is to use capital to generate not only financial wealth, but also human, social and societal benefits" (p. 41). More specifically, AXA reported on its commitment to all 17 SDGs but highlighted six of them – namely, SDGs 1, 3, 5, 9, 11 and 13.

Allianz, another leading international insurance company, claimed,

By the very nature of what we do – protecting people and businesses against risks – we contribute to our customers' long-term financial well-being and stabilizing local economies. Insurance is one of the key ways by which we limit the impacts of climate risks and compensate for climate-related damages. The higher the level of insurance coverage a country has, the more resilient it is to extreme natural events. Furthermore, following an extreme weather event such as a flood or hurricane, insurance payments are often a fast and reliable solution to help victims recover quickly, preventing them from falling into, or deeper into, poverty.

Allianz also claimed, "We are focused on supporting low-income customers in Asia, Africa and South America to close the gap for people who need access to low cost financial services" and that "digitalization is enabling more and more people to access insurance" (Allianz, 2017, p. 10).

More specifically, Allianz (2017) mapped its key activities and targets to the SDGs, and this in turn led to the identification of "the four SDGs to which we currently contribute to, and impact on, the most" (p. 9) – namely, SDGs 1, 7, 8 and 13. However, while the company targeted "four priority SDGs, our actual contribution is much wider" (p. 8). Here Allianz suggested,

> Given the nature and size of our business, we have the opportunity to impact many of the targets set by the SDGs. However, one of the complexities of the SDGs is their interconnectedness. You cannot single out one or two goals to which you solely contribute. In addition, our business activities and relationships are interconnected as well, which makes impact measurement challenging, be it positive or negative.
>
> *(p. 9)*

Deloitte (2015) expressed support for all 17 SDGs, noting that the company "is prepared to advance the SDGs across all five aspects of sustainable development, drawing on our recent work with clients" (p. 1). These five aspects are people, planet, prosperity, peace and partnerships. The company links each of the 17 SDGs to one of these five activity areas (SDGs 1–7 = people, SDGs 8–11 = prosperity, SDGs 12–15 = planet, SDG16 = peace, SDG17 = partnership) and then identifies how Deloitte's services are helping support their clients in each of the five areas. (Figure 1.1). Similarly, Credit Agricole (United Nations Global Compact, 2017) stated their support for SDGs 1–15, but to date, they have given little detail on how they will pursue this. In 2017, the group

> mapped several ongoing actions that might contribute towards the United Nations SDGs. Current discussions on the adaptation of CSR to all the business lines have revealed a need for greater clarity of the CSR strategy by focusing on three main areas: Ethics, Climate and Inclusion.
>
> *(Credit Agricole, 2019, para. 3)*

Actions and activities regarding specific SDGs

In addressing SDG1, AXA (2017) suggested that "an accident, illness or natural disaster can quickly plunge fragile populations into poverty," and reported that

People

We work with clients across sectors and geographies to help individuals live safer, healthier, more comfortable lives; from supporting the R&D capabilities of health providers to deploying technologies that expand water access to designing supportive structures for first generation college students.

Our services

Impact growth: **Assessing and visualizing which potential investments will generate the greatest impact to improving the quality of life for the world's poor.**

- Food security and agriculture: **Improving availability of agriculture inputs, building capacity to generate higher volumes and incomes and fostering sustainable agriculture and livelihoods.**
- Global health: **Implementing sustainable public and private programs to improve access to health care and wellness.**
- Education: **Addressing racial and socio-economic disparities in education through innovation and scaling solutions.**
- Diversity and Inclusion: **Helping organizations turn complexity into opportunity by recognizing the individual portfolio of strengths different individuals contribute and cultivating an accepting culture.**
- Water, energy and environment: **Supporting programs in renewable energy, water stewardship, access to safe water, sanitation and hygiene through innovative partnerships and technologies.**
- Anti-Human Trafficking: **Providing identity risk analytics to identify individuals potentially active in trafficking networks, as well as policy and regulatory planning and implementation to prevent trafficking.**

Prosperity

We understand that sustainable economic growth requires action across many dimensions and work with clients to advance a wide spectrum of market development and growth strategies.

Our services

- Social entrepreneurship and scaling: **Scaling impact through the development and implementation of innovative, effective organizational and field-level strategies. Core offerings include:**
  - **Regulatory, legal and policy reform and support**
  - **Sustainable financing**
  - **Transaction advisory and support**
- Strengthening livelihoods and job creation: **Improving the livelihoods of the world's poor through catalyzing investment in inclusive markets.**
- Improving capacity to govern: **Easing the challenges urbanization creates for cities and navigating the political environment to increase sustainable industrialization.**
- Impact measurement, evaluation and social return on investment: **Evaluating the impact of efforts to improve quality of life and livelihoods.**

FIGURE 1.1 Services offered by Deloitte for their people and prosperity areas of activity in support of the SDGs

Source: Deloitte, 2015, p. 2.

the company was "developing insurance products aimed at populations that do not have access to traditional insurance. Simpler, more flexible and more than just micro-insurance policies, these products form a safety net against poverty for these low-income populations" (p. 46). In focusing on its commitment to SDG13, the company reported,

> After divesting €500 million from the coal industry in 2015, AXA is com-
> mitted to increasing this divestment to €3 billion and to stop insuring coal
> construction projects. Similarly, AXA is making a €700 million divestment
> from oil sands producers and associated pipeline businesses, as well as a pledge

to stop insuring their activities. AXA also wants to create positive value in the fight against climate change and has increased its green investment targets to €12billion by 2020.

(p. 46)

Credit Suisse (2015) provided four case studies "to illustrate how our activities contribute to the realization of a number of specific SDGs and describe the measurable impact we aim to achieve" (p. 11). In addressing SDG8, for example, the bank argued that the company "had been a leader in microfinance since 2002" and that it "now offers additional impact funds" – for example, "a fair trade fund providing capital to agricultural cooperatives that support low-income farmers in developing countries" (p. 14). In outlining measurable impacts, Credit Suisse reported that some 85,000 fair-trade-oriented, small-scale farmers across 45 countries had received funding and that 58 company employees had worked onsite with local microfinance institutions. More recently (Credit Suisse, 2019), the bank noted it

> contributes to the realization of the SDGs in various ways, including in our role as a financial intermediary and employer. Further examples include our sustainable and impact investment products and services as well as our global initiatives in education and financial inclusion,

and "at the same time, our focus on sustainability risk management can help us to reduce potential negative impacts that certain business activities might have on the realization of the SDGs" (p. 9). The bank also gave details of its contribution to supporting its eight selected SDGs (Table 1.2).

In addressing SDG8, Allianz (2017) argued, "As one of the world's leading financial services providers, enabling sustainable economic growth is fundamental to our core business and provides a basis for delivering the SDGs" (p. 11). The company highlighted a number of projects that it suggested contributed to promoting inclusive and sustainable economic growth. These projects focussed on integrating environmental and social considerations into investment and insurance, fostering a work environment that includes inclusive meritocracy, supporting workplace health and well-being, protecting human rights and eliminating modern slavery in the supply chain and managing our environmental impacts to decouple economic growth from environmental degradation.

In support of SDG3 and SDG10, BNP Paribas (2018) are

> moving into social impact bonds. In Connecticut, we are working with the state government to fund local charities that support troubled families to keep children out of the care system. We get paid based on success – if a parent passes a drug test, for instance. The state saves money on its care bill but, more importantly, children from troubled families go on to lead better lives. We are going out to our clients across the spectrum, trying to figure out finance solutions to their sustainability challenges. We want to make it

TABLE 1.2 Credit Suisse: contribution to the realisation of the SDGs

Objective	Our contribution

Goal 4: Quality education

Ensure inclusive and equitable quality education and promote lifelong learning opportunities for all.	• We promote access to education and help to improve the quality of education through our Global Education Initiative. • We run a financial education programme for girls in Brazil, China, India, Rwanda, Sri Lanka and Tanzania. • We support regional education programmes in collaboration with partner organisations.

Goal 5: Gender equality

Achieve gender equality and empower all women and girls.	• We foster diversity and inclusion within our organisation. • We take measures to increase the proportion of women in management positions within our organisation. • We promote access to financial services for women in developing countries and emerging markets through our financial inclusion activities and run a financial education programme for girls.

Goal 7: Affordable and clean energy

Ensure access to affordable, reliable, sustainable and modem energy for all.	• We provide renewable energy financing. • We use climate-friendly energy sources for our business premises and have buildings certified according to energy efficiency standards. • We run an ISO 14001-certified environmental management system.

Goal 8: Decent work and economic growth

Promote sustained, inclusive and sustainable economic growth, full and productive employment and decent work for all.	• We offer progressive working conditions for our employees. • We support economic growth and entrepreneurship through our role as a lender and financial intermediary. • We are an integral part of the economy and society in our role as an employer, client, contractual partner and taxpayer. • We support an initiative to combat youth unemployment in Switzerland. • We help to strengthen local economies in developing countries and emerging markets through our activities in the area of financial inclusion.

Goal 9: Industry, innovation and infrastructure

Build resilient infrastructure, promote inclusive and sustainable industrialisation and foster innovation.	• We supply risk capital to support growth and innovator, including through Credit Suisse Entrepreneur Capital AG in Switzerland. • We help to strengthen local economies in developing countries and emerging markets through our activities in the area of financial inclusion. • We provide renewable energy financing. • We focus on sustainability risk management and have sector-specific policies and guidelines in place.

(*Continued*)

TABLE 1.2 (Continued)

Objective	Our contribution

Goal 11: Sustainable cities and communities

Make cites and human settlements inclusive, safe, resilient and sustainable.	• We invest in sustainable real estate. • We are committed to continuously improving the ESG performance (environmental, social and governance performance), energy efficiency and carbon footprint of our real estate investment portfolio.

Goal 13: Climate action

Take urgent action to combat climate change and its impacts.	• We are greenhouse gas neutral across all our operators globally. • We offer a range of green finance products and services for our clients. • We focus on sustainability risk management and have sector-specific policies and guidelines in place. • We seek to address the recommendations of the Financial Stability Board's Task Force on Climate-Related Financial Disclosures (FSB TCFD).

Goal 15: Life on land

Protect, restore and promote sustainable use of terrestrial ecosystems; sustainably manage forests; combat desertification; and halt and reverse landdegradation and halt biodiversity loss.	• We are active in the area of conservation finance. • We have an ongoing advisory role to the Sustainable Palm Oil Transparency Toolkit (SPOTT) and joined the Technical Advisory Group for the SPOTT timber, paper and pulp development. • We focus on sustainability risk management and have sector-specific policies and guidelines in place.

Source: Credit Suisse, 2019, p. 59.

financially viable for them to switch to sustainable practices and incentivise them for doing so. It makes us partners with clients on those projects and highlights the values we share in common.

(para. 8)

A number of elements are included in Citibank's commitment to enhancing the quality of life, the commercial strength of cities and urban resilience as an integral part of addressing SDGs 9 and 11. Citibank (2017) looks to harness

the powerful combination of our expertise in a wide range of areas such as bond issuances, digital payments and risk management to help urban leaders secure financing for infrastructure projects, find internal efficiencies to free up valuable resources, and leverage new technologies to automate and streamline service delivery.

(p. 14)

The digitisation of services is seen as an important opportunity, and Citibank (2017) reported "offering clients a range of digital solutions and services to meet their evolving financial needs" (p. 16). HSBC (2017) has used criteria related to the SDGs to determine eligibility for the bank's new style sustainable bond. There are two main considerations here: first, whether a business or project derives at least 90% of its revenues in the areas covered by selected SDGs and, second, whether a significant sustainability net impact is considered achievable. More specifically, the bank provides an indication of both the eligibility criteria and examples of potentially eligible projects for each of these seven SDGs. For SDG11, for example, the eligibility criteria are "activities that expand or maintain the supply of affordable housing" and "activities that expand or maintain access to sustainable transport systems" (p. 6), and examples include rail transport projects for public use, the development of roads in areas of poor accessibility and connectivity and the construction of social housing.

In outlining its contribution to SDGs 1 and 13, Allianz (2017) reported working with peer companies in the Insurance Development Forum to "pilot insurance approaches that allow governments in countries vulnerable to climate change to provide better shelter to their population" and to "participating in the Munich Climate Insurance Initiative to make more micro insurance solutions market ready for Caribbean countries" (p. 13). Similarly, in jointly addressing SDGs 7 and 13, Citibank (2017) focused on "financing the future we want" (p. 10) and "delivering on the SDGs" (p. 17). Financially, the company pledged to lend, invest and facilitate $100 billion to reduce the impacts of climate change with emphasis on renewable energy and energy efficiency projects, green buildings, water quality and conservation, clean technology, green bonds and sustainable transport. On delivery, the company provided two examples of its leadership in environmental finance – namely, its engagement in alternative energy finance and the growth of green bonds. Citibank (2017) reported "for alternative energy, we provide a range of financing solutions for environmental projects, including wind, solar, geothermal, bio mass, energy efficiency and other clean technologies" and "we offer construction financing, commodities hedging and tax equity, giving clients multiple services and a one stop shop for clients" (p. 12).

These initiatives in support of SDG13 resonate with statements made by the Bank of England (2018), which noted,

An important angle for the Bank of England is the risks that climate change poses for the stability of the financial system. Physical risks can arise from events like storms, floods and droughts. Meanwhile, transition risks can arise from changes in policy (such as the Paris Agreement) and technology (such as the growth of renewable energy).

(para. 7)

Scott, van Huizen and Jung (2017), from the Bank of England's Insurance and International Division, argued that climate change, and the responses to it, present two sets of financial risks which impact upon the Bank of England's objectives. These are "the physical effects of climate change and the impact of changes associated with the transition to a lower carbon economy" (para.1). Two principal elements were identified in the Bank of England's response to these risks: "engaging with firms which face current climate-related risks, such as segments of the insurance industry" and "enhancing the resilience of the UK financial system by supporting an orderly market transition" (p. 98). In conclusion, Scott et al. (2017) recognised that "responding to climate change will require many different actors to play a role" but suggested that the Bank of England was one of these in that it could help to ensure that "financial firms have considered climate-related financial risks and their role in supporting an orderly market transition" (p. 106).

Discussion

A number of issues are worthy of further discussion. First, there is a general consensus that the world's leading financial service companies have a vital role to play in contributing to achieving the SDGs. Ernst & Young (2015), for example, suggested that "the challenge for today's businesses is to address sustainability in a way that meets the current and future needs of their customers, employees, communities and the environment" and argued that "the financial services industry has a critical role to play in making this happen across both the public and private sectors" (p. 1) A number of the leading global companies within the financial services sector have publicly reported on how they plan to address the SDGs, often targeting specific SDGs where companies believe they can have the greatest impact. Other companies, however, seem to be slow to commit themselves publicly to the SDGs.

Second, there is some indication of a willingness amongst some financial services companies to take collaborative action to tackle the challenges posed by the SDGs, as evidenced by the UNEP Finance Initiative and the draft supervisory statement on managing the financial risks associated with climate change issued by the Bank of England Prudential Regulation Authority (2018). For example, in announcing its support for the UNEP Finance Initiative plan, Societe Generale (2018) claimed,

> The United Nations estimate that $US 5–7 trillion per year will be necessary to finance the 17 Sustainable Development Goals by 2030. Today, only a portion of these needs are covered, leaving a significant financing gap, and the private sector will play a key role in delivering these goals.
>
> *(para. 5)*

In a similar vein, BSR (2017), the global not-for-profit organisation, observed,

> It is estimated that the Sustainable Development Goals (SDGs), adopted in late 2015, will cost between US$90 trillion and US$120 trillion by 2030. In

this light, there is no doubt that the financial services industry has a role to play in funding the objectives

and concluded "there are many opportunities for investors and banks to fund the SDGs" (para.1).

Third, because of the nature of financial services, the industry can be seen as much a facilitator of change, as a leader or exemplar of such transition in its own company operations. It is thus important to distinguish between these two roles, although they can be seen as overlapping in some instances. For example, Ceres (2016), in proposing "a roadmap for sustainability" (para.1), suggested that the financial services industry can play a key role in supporting the move to a sustainable economy through its influence on capital across global markets but also reported that only a small number of financial services companies had to date demonstrated their commitment to sustainability. It remains to be seen to what extent the leading financial services companies will genuinely be prepared to collaborate and to coordinate their contributions to achieving the SDGs.

Conclusion

While there is a broad consensus that the financial services industry has a vital role to play in promoting sustainable development, there is a view that the industry could go further in proactively supporting and engaging with the SDGs. Stefanos Fatiou, chief of the Environment and Development Division at the UN Economic and Social Commission for Asia and the Pacific, argued, "If there is one sector we should ask more from, it's the finance sector" and added "if banks started using serious sustainability criteria in terms of how they evaluate loans and combine their portfolios, many changes would follow" (Sustainability, 2016, para.30).

Nevertheless, the companies reviewed in this chapter generally illustrated a positive, if evolving, approach to the SDGs in a period of upheaval and change due to the impact of new technology and increasing customer demands. Despite these pressures, given the scale of the challenges facing the successful achievement of the SDGs, the leading companies within the industry may well be advised to develop a coordinated and proactive approach and to communicate this approach effectively to all their stakeholders. As such, the financial services industry could be seen to be leading on, rather than reacting to, sustainability issues and to be proactively defining and providing solutions to these issues.

References

Allianz. (2017). *Responding to tomorrow's challenges: Allianz group sustainability report 2017*. Retrieved June 4, 2019, from www.allianz.com/content/dam/onemarketing/azcom/Allianz_com/investor-relations/en/results/2017-fy/180410-en-Sustainability-Report-2017.pdf

AXA. (2017). *In real life: 2017 integrated report*. Retrieved June 10, 2019, from https://www-axa-com.cdn.axa-contento-118412.eu/www-axa-com%2F2d414b6f-ac38-44ad-bf1d-0fc4b2a231f2_axa-ra2017-en-pdf-e-accessible_03.pdf

Bank of England. (2018). *Climate change: Why it matters to the bank of England.* Retrieved June 10, 2019, from www.bankofengland.co.uk/knowledgebank/climate-change-why-it-matters-to-the-bank-of-england

Bank of England Prudential Regulation Authority. (2018). *Enhancing banks' and insurers' approaches to managing the financial risks from climate change.* Consultation Paper 23. Retrieved June 10, 2019, from www.bankofengland.co.uk/-/media/boe/files/pruden tial-regulation/consultation-paper/2018/cp2318.pdf?la=en&hash=8663D2D47A725C 395F71FD5688E5667399C48E08

Barclays. (2019). *Supporting UN sustainable development goals.* Retrieved March 20, 2019, from https://home.barclays/news/2019/1/barclays-commits-to-un-sustainable-develop ment-goals/

BNP Paribas. (2018). *How financial services can support the sustainable development goals.* Retrieved March 22, 2019, from https://securities.bnpparibas.com/insights/sustainable-development-goals.html

BNP Paribas. (2019). *Corporate social responsibility.* Retrieved June 4, 2019, from https:// group.bnpparibas/en/group/corporate-social-responsibility

BSR. (2017). *Five ways the financial services industry can approach the sustainable development goals.* Retrieved October 11, 2018, from www.bsr.org/en/our-insights/blog-view/ five-ways-the-financial-services-industry-can-approach-the-sdgs

Ceres. (2016). *The Ceres roadmap for sustainability: Financial services.* Retrieved June 10, 2019, from www.ceres.org/roadmap-assessment/sector-analyses/financial-services

Citibank. (2017). *Banking on 2030: Citi and the sustainable development goals.* Retrieved May 25, 2019, from www.citigroup.com/citi/about/citizenship/download/Banking-on-2030-Citi-and-the-SDGs-Report.pdf?ieNocache=165

Credit Agricole. (2019). *Our CSR strategy: Partnering a sustainable economy.* Retrieved June 4, 2019, from www.credit-agricole.com/en/responsible-and-committed/our-csr-strategy-partnering-a-sustainable-economy

Credit Suisse. (2015). *Aiming for impact: Credit Suisse and the sustainable development goals.* Retrieved June 9, 2019, from https://sustainabledevelopment.un.org/content/ documents/2066cs-broschuere-aiming-forImpact-en.pdf

Credit Suisse. (2018). *Sustainable development goals.* Retrieved May 9, 2019, from www. credit-suisse.com/corporate/en/responsibility/approach-reporting/sustainable-develop ment-goals.html

Credit Suisse. (2019). *Corporate responsibility report 2018.* Retrieved May 25, 2019, from www. credit-suisse.com/media/assets/corporate/ . . . reports/csg-crr-2018-en.pdf

Deloitte. (2015). *How Deloitte supports the United Nations sustainable development goals.* Retrieved March 23, 2019, from https://www2.deloitte.com/content/dam/Deloitte/ global/Documents/About-Deloitte/gx_SDGs_Deloitte.pdf

Ernst & Young. (2015). *EMEIA financial services sustainability report 2015.* Retrieved June 10, 2019, from www.ey.com/Publication/vwLUAssets/ey-fostering-sustainability-in-finan cial-services/$FILE/ey-emeia-financial-services-sustainability-report-2014.pdf

HSBC. (2017). *HSBC sustainable development goal (SDG) bond framework.* Retrieved June 10, 2019, from www.hsbc.com/ . . . /pdfs/171115-hsbc-sdg-bond-framework.pdf .

HSBC. (2019). *Environmental, Social and Governance Update.* London: HSBC Holdings. Retrieved October 9, 2019, from https://www.hsbc.com › hsbc › pdfs › 190408-esg-update-april-2019-eng

One Stone Advisors. (2017). *The financial sector and the SDGs.* Retrieved May 19, 2019, from http://ethicalfinancehub.org/wp-content/uploads/2017/12/One-Stone-Financial-Sector-and-the-SDGs-WHITE-PAPER.pdf

Scholtens, B. (2006). Finance as a driver of corporate social responsibility. *Journal of Business Ethics*, *68*(1), 19–33.

Scott, M., van Huizen, J., & Jung, C. (2017). The bank of England's response to climate change. *Quarterly Bulletin Q2*, 97–108. ISSN 2399-4568. Retrieved October 18, 2018, from www.bankofengland.co.uk/quarterly-bulletin/2017/q2/the-banks-response-to-climate-change

Societe Generale. (2018). *Sustainable and positive impact finance*. Retrieved June 10, 2019, from https://wholesale.banking.societegenerale.com/en/solutions-services/sustainable-and-positive-impact-finance/

Standard Chartered Bank. (2019). *Sustainability aspirations 2019*. Retrieved March 26, 2019, from https://av.sc.com/corp-en/content/docs/sustainability-aspirations-2019.pdf

Sustainability. (2016). *Global trends and opportunities: 2016 and beyond*. Retrieved June 10, 2019, from http://radar.sustainability.com/annual-trends-report/

United Nations Environment Programme Finance Initiative. (2018). *Updated: 28 UNEP FI banking members working together to redefine how the banking industry delivers a sustainable future*. Retrieved May 19, 2019, from www.unepfi.org/news/industries/banking/principles-coregroup-announcement/

United Nations Global Compact. (2017). *Communication on progress – credit agricole S.A.* Retrieved May 7, 2019, from www.unglobalcompact.org/participation/report/cop/create-and-submit/active/323071

Weber, O., Diaz, M., & Schwegler, R. (2014). Corporate social responsibility of the financial sector – strengths, weaknesses and the impact on sustainable development. *Sustainable Development*, *22*(5), 321–335.

2

THE ICT INDUSTRY

Introduction

In 2008, the Global e-Sustainability Initiative (GeSI) reported on the contribution the ICT industry could make to sustainable development across a range of issues, including climate change, waste and material use; access to ICT; employee relationships; and economic development (GeSI, 2008). However, in looking to work "towards a new paradigm" for the relationship between "ICTs, the Internet and sustainable development," Souter, Maclean, Akoh and Creech (2010) stressed that there had been "surprisingly little interaction between policy makers and activists concerned with sustainable development and with ICT/Internet public policy" (p. 5). The problem was seen to reflect "the different interests of those concerned with sustainable development and with ICTs and internet public policy, and with the fact that the issues tend to be dealt with in different forums, among which there has been little interchange" (p. 5). Unwin (2015) highlighted how this gap between policy makers and the ICT industry was carried through in the formulation of the SDGs, as ICT is not mentioned in any of the 17 SDGs and is noted in just 4 of the 169 targets. He pointed out that "the almost complete omission of ICTs from the final agreed SDGs was a very serious failing" and that "those determining the SDG agenda for the next 15 years barely gave them any recognition at all" (p. 2).

There is a clear recognition of the difficulties involved in monitoring and measuring the impact of ICT, not least that there are a number of different ICTs with different impacts in different contexts and countries. Reports and materials relating to the SDGs from a range of ICT organisations are, therefore, reviewed, including major software companies (Microsoft and SAP), PC and electronics companies (Dell and Mitsubishi), hardware and services providers (Hewlett-Packard, Toshiba and Fujitsu), major telecommunications companies (Vodafone and Ericsson) and two industry bodies – *Groupe Speciale Mobile* Association (GSMA) and GeSI.

GSMA is a trade body that represents the interests of some 800 mobile telephone operators worldwide via industry programmes, working groups and industry advocacy initiatives. GeSI works in collaboration with members from world-leading ICT companies and organisations around the globe to offer information, resources and best practices for achieving integrated social and environmental sustainability through ICT.

Overview of the ICT industry and the SDGs

The company reports and related literature suggests that the ICT industry can play a central and vital role in contributing to the achievement of the SDGs. Dell (2017), for example,

> believes individual ICT providers will be important enablers of success, and . . . ICT will have a role to play in each of the Sustainable Development Goals. In some cases, ICT's role will be supportive. In others, however, that role will be primary and critical.
>
> *(p. 3)*

SAP (2018a), meanwhile, assert, "We are committed to these goals, and we invite you to join us through individual initiatives or partnerships" (para.5). Hans Vestberg, Ericsson's president and CEO, has argued, "Information Communication Technology offers an incredible platform for achieving the SDGs" (Ericsson and the Earth Institute Columbia University, 2016, p. 6), and Vodafone (2018) "is committed to leveraging the power of its technology, networks and services to contribute to these global goals" (p. 1).

More generally, GeSI (2016) argues, "Digital solutions from all areas of life can directly contribute to SDG achievements" and more pointedly that "digital solutions are indispensable, they transform the world quickly, with attractive propositions to people and with a positive impact to achieve all of the SDGs" (p. 3). In this context, SAP (2018a) suggests that their actions and activities support all the SDGs. They note,

> Our solutions help eradicate slavery from supply chains and document every living creature on the planet to protect endangered species. Experts use our data visualizations and analytics to help end deforestation, promote environmental awareness, and improve the quality of life everywhere. SAP software is helping to predict and prevent disasters, eliminate gender inequality, and educate people who have never had the chance to enter a classroom.
>
> *(para. 4)*

Microsoft (2017) stressed that the company sought "to apply the unique assets that a technology company of our scope and scale has towards the global multi-sector effort needed to achieve the SDGs" (p. 1). Ericsson and the Earth Institute

Columbia University (2016) visualised ICT as "a catalyst for achieving the SDGs" (p. 18) and argued that ICT, especially mobile broadband, will be the essential infrastructure platform for the SDGs and that "rapid action is needed to harness the contribution that ICT can make toward the achievement of the Global Goals" (p. 8). GSMA (2016) also observe that "all SDGs are impacted by the mobile industry to varying degrees" (p. 19).

However, the majority of ICT companies see their contribution as being primarily focussed on a more limited, but varied, range of the SDGs (Table 2.1). Fujitsu (2018), for example, note that "as a first step, using the digital technologies that are at the core of our business, we are focusing on five areas . . . in which we can deliver the greatest value" (para.5) and go on to identify SDGs 2, 3, 8, 9 and 11 as those where they can undertake specific initiatives. In a similar vein, Hewlett-Packard (2017) "supports the United Nations Sustainable Development Goals, and remains committed to driving progress on selected goals that are closely aligned to our Sustainable Impact strategy" (p. 26), and the company identifies SDGs 12 and 13 ("planet"), 5, 8 and 10 ("people") and 4 and 11 ("community") as those they can support and advance. Microsoft (2017) "prioritized eight SDGs to ensure we leverage our assets for the greatest impact," and the company has focussed its principal attention on SDGs 3, 4, 5, 8, 9, 11, 13 and 16, because of their "particular alignment with Microsoft's business and philanthropic strategies" (p. 1). Mitsubishi (2018) notes, "We believe we can make a contribution toward accomplishing the 17 globally shared goals of the SDGs" (para. 6), but that

> as a comprehensive electronics manufacturer, we can contribute significantly to Goal 7 "Affordable and clean energy," Goal 11 "Sustainable cities and communities," and Goal 13 "Climate action" . . . we will contribute even more to achieving the SDGs by creating value in these areas via technology synergies and business synergies and prioritizing the initiatives we advance.
>
> *(para. 7)*

Toshiba (2018) notes, "Our Carbon Zero programme supports 13 of the 17 Sustainable Development Goals set by the UN" (para. 1) and identify SDGs 1, 2, 3, 4, 5, 6, 8, 10, 12, 13, 15 and 17 as those they can support through specific actions and initiatives.

GSMA (2016) identified "the SDG targets that the mobile industry can impact in a significant way" (p. 17) – namely, SDGs 1, 4, 9 and 13. They argued that this choice "does not imply prioritisation on behalf of the industry"; rather, it reflects the SDGs, and associated targets, "that can currently be materially influenced by what the industry currently does" and "the importance of the industry to those targets" (p. 19). At the same time, they reported that it was also determined by the exclusion of those SDGs that emphasised state policy and/or intervention rather than the existence of a "compelling mobile industry driver" (p. 19). Vodafone (2018) notes that "through the impact of our extensive global network, wide range of products and services and the work of the Vodafone Foundation, we believe we

TABLE 2.1 SDGs addressed by ICT companies and organisations

SDG/ ICT company	Microsoft	Toshiba	Ericsson	Fujitsu	Hewlett-Packard	Vodafone	Mitsubishi	SAP	GSMA	GeSI
1		x	x					x	x	
2		x	x	x				x		
3	x	x	x	x				x		
4	x	x	x		x	x		x	x	
5	x	x	x		x	x		x		
6		x	x					x		x
7			x				x	x		x
8	x	x	x	x	x	x		x		
9	x		x	x		x		x	x	
10		x	x		x			x		
11	x		x	x	x		x	x		x
12		x	x		x			x		x
13	x	x	x		x	x	x	x	x	x
14			x					x		x
15		x	x					x		x
16	x		x					x		
17		x	x					x		

can have the greatest influence over the delivery of five of the UN SDGs" (p. 4), and identify SDGs 4, 5, 8, 9 and 13 as being of particular relevance to their business operations and aspirations. GeSI (2016) identified seven SDGs – namely, 6, 7, 11, 12, 13, 14 and 15 – as being focussed on protecting the environment while looking to ensure "that other goals are achieved without breaching the planet's ability to regenerate for future generations" (p. 26). Smart water management, for example, was identified as the most powerful digital solution to contribute to the achievement of SDG6, and here specific solutions included smart pipes, smart levees, smart metres, soil sensors, remote irrigation management, rain water harvesting systems, consumption control applications and e-billing. In addressing SDG12, the focus was on smart manufacturing and smart agriculture. The former included the industrial Internet of Things, three-dimensional printing, data analytics and cloud computing, drones and robotics and embedded system production technologies while the latter included automated irrigation systems and real time weather information, traceability and tracking systems. Ericsson and the Earth Institute Columbia University (2016) looked to demonstrate "the potential of ICT to drive progress on the SDGs" (p. 9) in four areas – namely, financial services, education, health, and energy and climate change.

Actions and activities regarding specific SDGs

Many ICT companies claim to be supporting the SDGs through sponsored projects to alleviate poverty, provide safe water and reduce carbon fuel emissions. Whilst a few examples of these initiatives are included here, the focus is more on how the technology itself can be used in support of the SDGs. As regards SDG1, GSMA (2016) maintains that the ICT industry plays an important role in helping to eradicate poverty and providing equal access to economic resources and building the resilience of the poor by "stimulating economic participation and activity through voice and data services, providing affordable connectivity, and acting as a provider of financial services to developing economies including the powerful platform of mobile remittances that is particularly valuable to underserved communities" (p. 19). Several of the companies reviewed made general statements in support of this goal. For example, Mitsubishi (2018) notes, "We are working to end poverty by creating employment through the global expansion of our business, and launching initiatives including the establishment of social infrastructure and philanthropic activities" (para.11). Similarly, as regards SDG2, Mitsubishi (2018) notes, "We are contributing to solving food-related issues through measures including the provision of IT support for agriculture via ICT and positioning satellites, improving productivity in foodstuffs factories through FA, and supplying refrigeration and freezing technologies for food" (para.12). In addressing SDG3, Microsoft (2017) reported on its role in providing products, services and training to help governments and health-care providers to "understand how to apply technologies like advanced data analytics and cloud solutions to transform healthcare" (p. 4). Fujitsu (2018) also identify a number of initiatives they are making in support of SDG2 and SDG3 (Figure 2.1).

For SDG4, GSMA (2016, p. 19) suggests that the ICT industry can provide connectivity to schools and access to educational platforms and facilitate the purchase of school-related services in less developed economies. This is borne out by Hewlett-Packard (2017), who note that

> HP is building effective and innovative education solutions for millions of people worldwide, including women and girls, and under-represented and marginalized groups. Our goal is to enable better learning outcomes for 100 million people by 2025, since the beginning of 2015, by deploying breakthrough technology solutions that support engaging, personalized educational experiences; partnering to develop scalable models for digital inclusion and lifelong learning; and delivering insights that help governments create effective education and human capital development policies and programs.
>
> *(p. 27)*

Similarly, Vodafone (2018) have made the commitment "to support 10 million young people to access digital skills, learning and employment opportunities by 2022. The Vodafone Foundation aims to provide up to 5 million young refugees, particularly girls, with access to a digital education by 2020" (p. 3).

Impact			Our initiative (examples)
SDG2		**Sustainable Food and Agriculture** Increase food productivity and resilience	• Over 400 businesses in Japan use Fujitsu's agriculture cloud service Akisai to increase productivity. It is also available in other countries like Vietnam. • We are operating our own precision agriculture facility and collaborating in smart agriculture with diverse industry partners.
SDG3		**Wellbeing of People** Realize a high quality of life for everyone in an aging society, and eradicate difficult diseases by medical innovation	• Fujitsu connected 7,000 hospitals, clinics, care facilities and pharmacies to help realize wellbeing for everyone. • We co-created sensor-based monitoring services for patients and elderly people in Netherland and Singapore. • We are also collaborating with various research institutions in genome-based medicine and drug discovery, using our HPC and AI technologies.
SDG8		**Decent Work and Sustainable Economic Growth** Accelerate innovation and realize a human-centric way to work	• Fujitsu helps organizations transform their ways of working, enabling their people to work more creatively with the support of Human Centric AI. • We provide a voice recognition end AI-based 19-language translation tool to support communications between diverse people including the hearing-impaired. • We are actively accelerating open innovation with start-ups.
SDG9		**Sustainable Industrialization** Realize intelligent industrialization through innovation	• Fujitsu provides an industry platform to help manufacturing companies digitalize their businesses and accelerate intelligent industrialization through co-creation. • We are supporting smart manufacturing in China and Singapore and digital innovation in France. • We are also supporting the development of digital talent, for instance, through our Digital Business College.
SDG11		**Sustainable City** Enable intelligent mobility, and increase safety and resilience to disasters	• Fujitsu co-created innovative services with many organizations, using our location information cloud service SPATIOWL as a platform for mobility. • We are jointly developing innovative solutions for urban challenges in Singapore. • We globally provide HPC- based disaster prediction solutions as well as solutions to prevent and mitigate the damages by earthquakes, tsunamis and floods. • UN Development Programme, Tohoku University and Fujitsu jointly developed a global database of disasters.

FIGURE 2.1 Fujitsu: specific SDGs advanced by company initiatives

Source: Fujitsu, 2018, para. 6.

With reference to SDG5, Hewlett-Packard (2017) notes,

> We work to grow the pipeline of diverse talent and to recruit and develop female and diverse talent across all levels of the company. We also use our scale to influence our suppliers and partners, encouraging them to prioritize diversity and inclusion within their own operations.
>
> *(p. 27)*

Vodafone (2018) has committed

> to connect an additional 50 million women living in emerging markets to mobile. We aim to improve the lives of millions of women by using our technology to enable greater access to financial inclusion; improve health and wellbeing; and build skills and entrepreneurship. We champion the inclusion of women in the workplace and aim to become the best employer for women globally by 2025.
>
> *(p. 3)*

For SDG6, Mitsubishi (2018) notes, "The Group has technology for treating and purifying water, and supplies technologies and systems whose purpose is to deliver safe water" (para.15), and SAP (2018b) cites a number of water related companies and authorities who are using their systems. The company notes that they are

> proud to help companies such as Vectus and the Cities of Capetown and Antibes and to partner with others like Viva con Agua and Itron to address the world's water and sanitation challenges . . . we're also proud to say we are reducing our water footprint in facilities around the world through the adoption of waterless bathroom fixtures and the use of gray water where possible. Together, we can ensure safe water for everyone on earth.
>
> *(para.18)*

For SDG7, Mitsubishi (2018) claims to be "working to develop technologies and systems that will help produce a smart, energy-conserving, and energy-creating society – technologies, products, and services that we are endeavoring to make widely available" (para.16).

In addressing SDG8, Microsoft states that they are working with a global spread of governments, development agencies and non-governmental organisations to promote economic development and to empower entrepreneurs and business leaders with the tools, skills and opportunities to stimulate and facilitate economic growth. As illustrative examples of its work, Microsoft (2017) cites "Kenya AGIN," which is a cloud-based service which uses farmer profile and production data to help farmers establish their creditworthiness and its work with India's Ministry of

Rural Development to develop a skills matching and payments solutions to help some 128 million workers find employment. Hewlett-Packard (2017) state,

> We forbid any forced, bonded, or indentured labor, involuntary prison labor, slavery, or trafficking of persons within our supply chain, and have adopted a broad approach to the topic of responsible minerals sourcing to help ensure there is no connection between the materials used in HP products and armed violence or human rights abuses.
>
> *(p. 27)*

Vodafone (2018) aims to "support 10 million young people to access digital skills, learning and employment opportunities by 2022. As an employer, we aim to provide up to 100,000 young people with a digital workplace experience at Vodafone by 2022" (p. 3). Dell (2017) has identified SDG8 for particular support and has

> launched EntrepreneursUNite in collaboration with the UN Foundation to ensure that SDG8 is recognized as a priority by all Member States in the post-2015 development agenda. As the number one creators of new jobs, entrepreneurs and small businesses are the engine driving the global economy. EntrepreneursUNite is a movement to help entrepreneurs scale globally to create the jobs the world needs and advance the greatest innovations of our time.
>
> *(para. 1)*

As regards SDG9, Vodafone (2018) notes that by extending their networks "to connect the unconnected and improve broadband access, we aim to enhance global communications infrastructure and the opportunities that flow from greater connectivity" (p. 3) (Figure 2.2). Indeed, "connecting the unconnected" (Ericsson and the Earth Institute Columbia University, 2016, p. 24) is universally seen as being a critical component that the ICT industry can make in the achievement of the SDGs. Fujitsu (2018), for example, suggests that "the SDGs are one element in an ecosystem aimed at achieving the Fujitsu growth strategy of 'connected services', pointing the way to new business opportunities through ventures that work to resolve social issues" (para.3). GSMA (2016) stressed the importance of "extending network coverage to rural areas" but arguably more importantly recognised that while connectivity "is a very important first step" the real prize is about "what this connectivity enables" namely "connecting everyone and everything to a better future" (p. 5).

In terms of SDG10, Hewlett-Packard (2017)

> strives to uphold fundamental rights and freedoms of all people. We promote a welcoming, diverse, and inclusive culture and do not tolerate discrimination of any kind. Through leading policies, programs, and partnerships, we aim to promote social and economic inclusion for all people across our supply

9 INDUSTRY INNOVATION
AND INFRASTRUCTURE

Build resilient infrastructure, promote sustainable industrialisation and foster innovation

Vodafone's commitments

By extending Vodafone's networks to connect the unconnected and improve broadband access, we aim to enhance global communications infrastructure and the opportunities that flow from greater connectivity.

13 CLIMATE
ACTION

Take urgent action to combat climate change and its impacts

Vodafone's commitments

To reduce our greenhouse gas emissions by 40%.

To purchase 100% of the electricity we use from renewable sources.

To continue to ensure our IoT products and services play a significant role in helping customers to reduce their greenhouse gas emissions.

FIGURE 2.2 Vodafone's commitment to SDGs 9 and 13

Source: Vodafone, 2018, p. 4.

chain and operations – regardless of race, ethnicity, gender, nationality, ability, military status, religion, generation, sexual orientation, or views.

(p. 27)

For SDG11, Hewlett-Packard (2017) states that they

aim to make a positive local impact on the communities where HP employees, customers, and suppliers live, work, and do business. We provide financial support for communities affected by natural disasters and emergencies, and work with expert partners to speed recovery and reconnect vital networks. HP employees also contribute their talents, passions, and resources to support inclusive, safe, resilient, and sustainable communities worldwide.

(p. 27)

As regards SDG12, there are examples from a number of ICT companies that have sponsored projects in support of this goal. The Toshiba CarbonZero Scheme, for example,

supports the ongoing activities to rehabilitate and maintain boreholes in Uganda. These are mainly boreholes which have fallen into disrepair, denying communities access to safe water and forcing people to burn firewood in order to boil water to make it safe, thereby contributing to CO_2 emissions.

(Toshiba, 2017, para.3)

More specifically, Hewlett-Packard (2017) "aim[s] to develop solutions that keep materials in use at their highest state of value for the longest possible time, grow the market for recycled content, and offer robust repair, reuse, and recycling programs for our products worldwide" (p. 27).

With the exception of Fujitsu, all the organisations reviewed specifically identify SDG13 as a priority. Vodafone (2018), for example, notes as their objectives regarding SDG13:

To reduce our greenhouse gas emissions by 40%; to purchase 100% of the electricity we use from renewable sources; to continue to ensure our IoT products and services play a significant role in helping customers to reduce their greenhouse gas emissions.

(p. 3)

Similarly, Hewlett-Packard (2017) asserts that the company "is driving progress toward our goals to reduce GHG emissions across our value chain and . . . we continue to support coordinated global action to combat climate change." They state that they are "investing in energy efficiency and shifting toward less GHG-intensive energy sources, including on- and off-site renewable power, with the goal of reaching 100% renewable electricity use in our global operations" (p. 27).

GeSI (2016) took a slightly different approach and identified three of the targets under SDG13, which they considered the most likely to benefit from digital solutions. These were strengthening resilience and adaptive capacity to climate-related hazards and natural disasters, integrating climate change measures into national policies and planning and improving educational awareness and human and institutional capacity on climate change mitigation. Indeed, they argued "luckily digital solutions have an enormous potential to reduce greenhouse gas emissions" and suggested that "smart manufacturing, smart agriculture, smart buildings, smart mobility and smart energy" could cut global greenhouse gas emissions by some 20% by 2030. Arguably more tellingly, they also suggested that "these digital solutions can help us to hold emissions at current levels while enabling the huge strides in equitable growth and quality of life" and optimistically further suggested that "at the very least, digital solutions can help us to stabilize global climatic conditions that are recognizable today – while enabling economic growth to do its work in lifting people out of poverty" (p. 29). Microsoft (2017) reported on its carbon neutrality strategy and on achieving carbon neutrality spanning over 100 countries in its data centres, software development labs, offices and company owned manufacturing plants. The company's carbon neutrality strategy is underpinned by a "chargeback model," which "puts a price on carbon and makes the company's business divisions responsible for the cost of reducing and compensating for carbon emissions associated with their electricity use and air travel," while the resultant "carbon fee funds energy efficient investments" (p. 17). The project ensures that communities have all the timesaving and health benefits of a safe water supply but goes further by putting structures in place to ensure the responsible use of this vital resource.

There is relatively little specific reference in the available ICT literature to SDGs 14, 15 or 16. Regarding SDG14 and SDG15, Mitsubishi (2018) notes that "we develop and supply observation satellites that deliver information about ocean and forest conditions, and furthermore promote initiatives at our offices aimed at harmonizing their activities with the local environment" (para.24). SAP (2018c) cites a number of organisations that use their systems to address SDG15. They note, for example, that "SAP technology is helping the DOC, Barcode of Life, LifeScanner, Elephants, Rhinos & People (ERP) and indigenous people of the Amazon as they enable others to do their part in preserving the world's biodiversity" (para.26).

SDG17 is referred to in several company reports, both in terms of technology deployment to support the goal and as regards the actions of the companies in partnership development and management. SAP (2018d), for example, states that the company "is working hard to revitalize the partnerships needed to achieve the UN's global goals," and that

> as part of SAP's cooperation with UNIDO and its membership in the Global Partnership for Sustainable Development Data, we are using our analytics expertise and technology to help UNIDO engage in guiding governments around the world through data-driven discussions . . . methods include utilizing innovative technologies, such as analytics, reporting, the Internet of Things, and artificial intelligence. The first milestone is the development of an innovative platform, SAP Digital Boardroom, to monitor, manage, and report on the sustainable development goals, especially SDG 9 – related data and targets.
>
> *(SAP, 2018d, para. 15)*

Several other companies make more general statements, such as Mitsubishi (2018), which asserts, "We are contributing to the achievement of the SDGs through partnerships with entities including governments, universities, research institutes, companies, and NGOs, pushing ahead with open innovation and other initiatives" (para.27).

Discussion

The ICT industry has been keen to emphasise what it sees as its key role in contributing to the achievement of the SDGs, and a number of issues merit further discussion. First, the ICT industry sees the SDGs as a major new business opportunity. Under the banner "Sustainable Development Makes Good Business Sense," GeSI (2016) claimed that "the digital solutions that catalyse SDG achievement" could generate "$3.1 trillion of additional annual revenue to the sector, from rolling out a range of established and emerging technologies across all markets" (p. 32), representing a growth boost of 60% to the ICT industry. A focus on the business opportunities for the ICT industry associated with the SDGs might be seen to resonate with the concept of shared value. For Huawei, for example, the SDGs are viewed as "a framework that we could use to reposition our strategy . . . and maximize the role of technology in addressing the goals." The company aims "to convince western consumers it is serious about sustainability" as part of its strategy to "connect the World and take on Apple" (Balch, 2018, para.18).

Second, there is a recognition that the role and the impact of the ICT industry in contributing to the SDGs will vary in different parts of the world. Generally, this is implicitly recognised in discussing the different potential for impact in urban and rural areas and between developed and less developed economies. More explicitly, GSMA (2016) reported on variations in the future opportunities for the mobile industry to impact on economies at different stages of development and in different geographic regions. In addressing the former, they reported (p. 73) that within "developed" economies the mobile industry would have a high impact on SDGs 13, 5 and 11. In contrast, they suggested (p. 74) that the overall impact of mobile industry within "developing" economies will be lower than the global average and that would be most marked in relation to SDGs 13 and 7. By way of contrast, within Europe, the impact of the mobile industry is seen to be high across most of the SDGs, but the GSMA report (2016) suggested that there is scope to increase the impact on SGD17 through the ICT industry's leadership of "multi-stakeholder partnerships, driving co-ordination of the sustainable development agenda, as well as continuing to develop and implement open platforms that enable innovation ecosystems and provide a blueprint for other regions to follow" (p. 79).

Third, there are a range of barriers and challenges that need to be addressed if the ICT industry is to play a full role in contributing to the achievement of the SDGs. Ericsson and the Earth Institute Columbia University (2016) identified a number of "practical hurdles" (p. 16) to the effective widespread deployment of

ICT in helping to achieve the SDGs. These hurdles included public-sector regulation, which does not yet enable full utilisation of ICT; the need for rapid expansion and upgrading of wireless broadband particularly in rural areas; the training of personnel to operate and manage ICT systems; and the incubation of new ICT start-ups. Governments clearly have a vital enabling role in allowing the industry to make that contribution. Dell (2017), for example, "expects major SDG initiatives to be driven primarily at governmental or intergovernmental levels . . . governmental efforts will frequently need to partner or collaborate with the commercial sector in order to have maximum effect" (p. 2). However, there appear to be contradictions in the policy role the ICT industry would like to see governments playing. On the one hand, GeSI (2016) has called upon governments to play "their part in shaping policy and legal frameworks" by "liberalising some markets, improving the ease of doing business and bearing down on restrictive practices" (p. 36) and thereby reducing the regulatory role of the state. On the other hand, the ICT industry is generally united in calling for government investment in wholesale improvements in connectivity in less developed economies.

Fourth, there are arguably more fundamental tensions between the ICT industry's commitments to future growth and the achievement of the SDGs. Some companies have linked the pursuit of the SDGs to their CSR and corporate governance activities. Mitsubishi (2018), for example, notes,

> We will specify and revise our CSR materiality with a focus on how we can contribute to resolving social issues as a company, and seek to contribute to realizing the SDGs through the initiatives we apply to the CSR materiality.
>
> *(para. 9)*

However, others adopt a more growth-oriented perspective. GSMA (2016), in addressing SDG7, looked to "sustain per capita economic growth in accordance with national circumstances and, in particular, at least 7 per cent gross domestic product growth per annum in the least developed countries" (p. 165). However, many critics argue that such growth will make increasingly severe demands on the Earth's finite natural resources, and there are concerns that these demands and the continuing corporate commitment to growth that drive them will prove ultimately unsustainable.

Fifth, the nature and impact of ICTs is rapidly evolving, and the pace of change will increase further in the period up to 2030 (Wynn & Jones, 2020). Ericsson and the Earth Institute Columbia University (2016) argued, "ICTs have the potential to increase the rate of diffusion of a very wide range of technologies across the economy" and "the accelerated up take of these technologies . . . constitute the key to achieving the SDGs by their target date of 2030" (p. 12). The unprecedented nature and pace of technology development might be seen to offer sustainable solutions to seemingly elusive environmental and social challenges and might thus allow the ICT industry to make a major and lasting contribution to the SDGs. Heeks (2014), for example, noted that ICT products and services that are currently in the fore for use in developing countries are "near-ubiquity of mobile, spread of broadband, more big/open/real-time data, use of field sensors/embedded computing, more social media, more crowd-sourcing models, more cloud, more smartphones, and 3D printing" (p. 2), but that the scope, reach and depth of ICTs in developing countries is changing pace. He concluded, "The relationship between digital ICTs and international development can be divided into three paradigms – pre-digital, ICT4D, and digital development" (Heeks, 2017a, para.1). The digital paradigm is now on the ascent and will overtake the ICT4D paradigm by 2030.

In practice, this means that the nature and potential impact of ICT solutions in support of the SDGs will take increasingly new forms in the years up to 2030 as new digital platforms become available. Heeks (2017b) notes, "We can therefore think of three generations of technological infrastructure for digital development." The first "already well-rooted, is based largely around mobile devices. The second, currently emerging, is based around digital platforms and the Internet including Web 2.0 applications. The third, currently nascent, will be based around a ubiquitous computing model of sensors, embedded processing and near-universal connectivity, and widespread use of smart applications" (para.7). ICTs are, therefore, evolving in developing countries from "a specialist tool to an everyday utility with digital mediation, emerging as the dominant mechanism for many processes of economic, political and cultural development" (Heeks, 2016, p. 8). Given some of the preceding discussion and the general absence of ICT concepts and actions in the SDGs, such a transformation may appear questionable. But the technological developments of the last 30 years and the increasing pace of change suggests Heeks' assertions are likely to prove correct, placing even more focus on the role of the ICT sector in support of the SDGs. ICTs may no longer be "just tools to enable particular aspects of development, but the platform that mediates development" (Heeks, 2016, p. 1).

Conclusion

At the closing of the 2018 High-Level Political Forum on Sustainable Development, UN secretary-general Antonio Guterres concluded "technology has great potential to help deliver the SDGs," and "we need to harness the benefits of advanced technologies for all" (United Nations Secretary-General, 2018, para.27). Certainly, the ICT industry has stressed that it believes it has a vital role to play in driving progress towards the global transformation that the SDGs demand but monitoring and evaluating the role of the ICT industry in contributing to the achievement of the SDGs is likely to be a complex and contested process.

The ICT industry has identified the SDGs as a massive business opportunity, and the industry is looking to develop what GSMA (2016) described as the "coordination and standardisation of the industry's messages globally" which is seen to be "critical to achieve optimal results for all stakeholders" (p. 98). This is particularly significant as "the deployment of new technologies could be essential for achieving the SDGs, considering the need for accelerated progress to fulfil the goals by 2030"

(Diplo, 2018, para.13). In this context, the ICT industry has emphasised the vital importance of the role of governments in creating a more liberal market environment and in funding many of the necessary improvements in connectivity. Looking to the future, the role of governments, particularly in less developed economies, in effectively addressing these challenges may prove problematic, although the rapid pace of technological development within the ICT industry may revolutionise how the SDGs can be achieved.

References

Balch, O. (2018). *Global goals: Huawei's strategy to connect the world – and take on apple.* Retrieved October 16, 2018, from www.ethicalcorp.com/global-goals-huaweis-strategy-connect-world-and-take-apple

Dell. (2017). *Dell and the United Nation's sustainable development goals.* Retrieved October 16, 2018, from www.businessfor2030.org/dell/

Diplo. (2018). *Digital technology for the sustainable development goals.* Retrieved June 19, 2019, from www.diplomacy.edu/blog/digital-technology-sdgs

Ericsson and the Earth Institute Columbia University. (2016). *ICT & SDGs: Final report.* Retrieved June 20, 2019, from www.ericsson.com/assets/local/news/2016/05/ict-sdg.pdf

Fujitsu. (2018). *SDG-related activities in Fujitsu.* Retrieved October 16, 2018, from www.fujitsu.com/global/about/csr/vision/sdgs/

GeSI (Global e-Sustainability Initiative). (2008). *The contribution the ICT industry can make to sustainable development.* Retrieved January 23, 2017, from http://gesi.org/files/Reports/The%20Contribution%20the%20ICT%20Industry%20Can%20Make%20to%20Sustainable%20Development.pdf

GeSI (Global e-Sustainability Initiative and Accenture Strategy). (2016). *System transformation: How digital solutions will drive progress towards the sustainable development goals.* Retrieved August 23, 2018, from http://systemtransformation-sdg.gesi.org/160608_GeSI_System Transformation.pdf

GSMA (*Groupe Speciale Mobile* Association). (2016). *2016 mobile industry impact report: Sustainable development goals.* Retrieved May 15, 2018, from www.gsma.com/betterfuture/wp-content/uploads/2016/09/_UN_SDG_Report_FULL_R1_WEB_Singles_LOW.pdf

Heeks, R. (2014). ICT4D 2016: New priorities for ICT4D policy, practice and WSIS in a post- 2015 world. *Development informatics.* Working Paper Series, No. 59. Retrieved May 5, 2018, from http://hummedia.manchester.ac.uk/institutes/gdi/publications/workingpapers/di/di_wp59.pdf

Heeks, R. (2016). Examining digital development: The shape of things to come. *Development informatics.* Working Paper Series, No. 63. Retrieved May 4, 2018, from https://mecon.nomadit.co.uk/pub/conference_epaper_download.php5?PaperID

Heeks, R. (2017a). *An emerging digital development paradigm.* Retrieved March 21, 2017, from http://blog.gdi.manchester.ac.uk/emerging-digital-development-paradigm/

Heeks, R. (2017b). *Technological foundations for digital development.* Retrieved March 21, 2017, from https://ict4dblog.wordpress.com/author/richardheeks/

Hewlett-Packard. (2017). *HP 2017 sustainable impact report.* Retrieved November 8, 2018, from https://h20195.www2.hp.com/V2/getpdf.aspx/c05179523.pdf

Microsoft. (2017). *Microsoft and the UN sustainable development goals.* Retrieved May 23, 2018, from download.microsoft.com/ .../Microsoft%20and%20the%20UN%20SDGs%20Sept%20. . .

Mitsubishi. (2018). *CSR materiality and SDGs management*. Retrieved October 16, 2018, from www.mitsubishielectric.com/en/sustainability/csr/management/management/materiality_sdgs/index.html

SAP. (2018a). *17 global goals to achieve a sustainable future*. Retrieved October 16, 2018, from www.sap.com/dmc/exp/2018-01-unglobalgoals/

SAP. (2018b). *17 global goals to achieve a sustainable future – goal 6: Clean water and sanitation*. Retrieved November 27, 2018, from www.sap.com/dmc/exp/2018-01-unglobalgoals/6_Clean_Water_Sanitation.html

SAP. (2018c). *17 global goals to achieve a sustainable future – goal 15: Life on land*. Retrieved November 27, 2018, from www.sap.com/dmc/exp/2018-01-unglobalgoals/15_Life_on_Land.html

SAP. (2018d). *17 global goals to achieve a sustainable future – goal 17: Partnerships for the goals*. Retrieved November 27, 2018, from www.sap.com/dmc/exp/2018-01-unglobalgoals/17_Partnerships_for_the_Goals.html

Souter, D., Maclean, D., Akoh, B., & Creech, H. (2010). *ICTs, the internet and sustainable development: Towards a new paradigm*. Retrieved January 23, 2017, from www.iisd.org/sites/default/files/publications/icts_internet_sd_new_paradigm.pdf

Toshiba. (2017). *Toshiba carbon zero scheme (SDG12)*. Toshiba Tec Germany Imaging Systems GmbH.

Toshiba. (2018). *Supporting the United Nations*. Retrieved November 11, 2018, from www.toshibatec.eu/campaigns/un-sustainable-development-goals/

United Nations Secretary-General. (2018). *Remarks at closing of high-level political forum on sustainable development*. Retrieved June 19, 2018, from www.un.org/sg/en/content/sg/speeches/2018-07-18/hlpf-sustainable-development-closing-remarks

Unwin, T. (2015). *ICTs and the failure of the sustainable development goals*. Retrieved January 23, 2017, from https://unwin.wordpress.com/2015/08/05/icts-and-the-failure-of-the-sustainable-development-goals/

Vodafone. (2018). *Our contribution to the UN SDGs: Vodafone*. Retrieved November 14, 2018, from www.vodafone.com/content/dam/vodafone-images/sustainability/downloads/sdgs.pdf

Wynn, M., & Jones, P. (2020). The sustainable development goals, the ICT industry and ICT4D research. In T. Keong, P. Flynn, & M. Gudic (Eds.), *Struggles and success in the pursuit of sustainable development*. Oxford: Routledge.

3

THE AUTOMOTIVE INDUSTRY

Introduction

In 2016, the automotive industry contributed a turnover of £77.5 billion to the UK economy, the highest figure on record for the United Kingdom, and "continued to advance its sustainability . . . making gains in productivity, economic contribution and environmental impact" (SMMT News, 2017, para.2). Although vehicle production was up 8.9%, energy use, water use and waste to landfill was reduced. "The sector's improved social and economic performance was achieved while simultaneously reducing the environmental impact of its manufacturing processes" (SMMT News, 2017, para.8). Yet the industry is in the throes of major evolution of its core products. In the period leading up to 2030, Bell (cited in National Instruments, 2018) suggests that "within the next 10 years, we will see remarkable change in the automotive industry . . . from improved engine efficiency to autonomous vehicles to electrification" (p. 2). The automotive industry, both in the United Kingdom and worldwide, can thus play a critical role in the pursuit of many of the SDGs, and this chapter assesses the attitude and commitment of some of the industry's main players regarding the realisation of the SDGs.

The companies reviewed in this chapter are Nissan, a Japanese multinational automobile manufacturer headquartered in Nishi-ku, Yokohama; Toyota, another Japanese multinational automotive manufacturer headquartered in Toyota, Aichi, Japan; Honda Motor Company, a Japanese public multinational conglomerate corporation, which manufactures both automobiles and motorcycles and has its headquarters in Tokyo; Ford Motor Company, founded by Henry Ford in 1903 and now an American multinational with its main headquarters in Detroit; General Motors, another American multinational corporation that designs, manufactures, markets and distributes vehicles and vehicle parts, and is also headquartered in Detroit; Volvo, a Swedish automobile company, with headquarters in Gothenburg, but now owned by Chinese automotive company Geely; Daimler, a German multinational automotive company, headquartered in Stuttgart; Audi, another German automobile manufacturer, now a member of the Volkswagen Group; BMW, a German multinational company which makes both automobiles and motorcycles and is headquartered in Munich; and Fiat Chrysler, an Italian–American multinational corporation with its headquarters in London. The activities of some other companies – Jaguar and Hyundai, for example – are also noted in certain sections.

Overview of the automotive industry and the SDGs

In either their annual company reports or sustainability reports, nearly all the major automobile companies studied here make specific reference to their contributions or actions in support of some of the SDGs (Table 3.1). General Motors has arguably the most comprehensive approach. In the company's *2017 Sustainability Report* (General Motors, 2017a), General Motors explains how "our sustainability initiatives intersect the 17 goals outlined in the 2030 agenda for sustainable development" (para.1). Somewhat similarly, Nissan's *2018 Sustainability Report* (Nissan, 2018), the company notes, "The automobile industry . . . faces an increasingly important responsibility to provide value to society by delivering safe, secure and sustainable mobility for all" (contribution to SDGS, para.1). For all 17 SDGs, the company identifies specific goal targets, and Nissan's contribution and approach to them. Although the company supports all the SDGs, it identifies indicators for its own performance for SDGs 3, 5, 6, 7, 8, 12, 13 and 16, and reports on results year by year starting in 2015 for each of these. The company's approach and performance indicators for SDGs 12 and 13, for example, are shown in Table 3.2.

Fiat Chrysler Automobiles (FCA) takes an equally wide-ranging approach, noting, "Our global activities support the transition toward a circular economy and contribute to achieving the aims of the United Nations Sustainable Development Goals" (Fiat Chrysler Automobiles Group, 2017, para.7). Their *2017 Sustainability Report* "provides concrete evidence of FCA's sustainability commitment and our alignment with the principles of the United Nations 2030 Agenda and the following Sustainable Development Goals: 3–13" (para.10). The company maps its "material sustainability topics" (Fiat Chrysler Automobiles Group, 2018, p. 13) against these 11 SDGs (Table 3.3).

Other companies have taken a somewhat more targeted approach. Ford, for example, notes that the company "contributes toward meeting those SDGs that most directly relate to our business and where we can add most value" (Ford Motor Company, 2018, para.3) and identified SDGs 3, 6, 9, 11, 12 and 13 as priorities. Volvo similarly states that "our ambition is to contribute to all SDGs in our activities, but to focus on those most relevant for our business where we can contribute the most" (Volvo Group, 2017, para.2). For the Volvo Group, this means focusing on SDGs 3, 9, 11 and 13. Honda (2018) came to a similar conclusion through the development of a "materiality matrix" in which

issues were identified through dialogue among members of respective operating divisions within the Company and the process took into account

TABLE 3.1 SDGs addressed by automobile companies

SDG/ auto company	Ford	Volvo	Daimler	Fiat Chrysler	Audi	BMW	Honda	General Motors	Toyota	Nissan
1								x		
2								x		
3	x	x		x			x	x	x	x
4				x	x			x		
5				x				x		x
6	x			x				x		x
7				x			x	x		x
8			x	x	x			x		x
9	x	x	x	x				x		
10				x				x		
11	x	x	x	x		x		x	x	
12	x		x	x	x	x		x		x
13	x	x	x	x	x	x	x	x	x	x
14								x		
15								x		
16								x		x
17								x		

various viewpoints including global and value chain perspectives, the status of technological innovation, Sustainable Development Goals and social issues pursuant to the Paris Agreement.

This analysis led them to conclude that

> our efforts should contribute to the achievement of certain SDGs, notably Goal 13 "Take urgent action to combat climate change and its impacts"; Goal 7 "Ensure access to affordable, reliable, sustainable and modern energy for all"; and Goal 3 "Ensure healthy lives and promote well-being for all at all ages."
>
> *(p. 16)*

In their 2017 *Annual Report*, Toyota (2017) report that the company is

> utilizing its strengths to help solve global social problems in line with the United Nations SDGs, promulgated in January 2016. In addition to addressing climate change (in line with SDG13), Toyota is working to reduce traffic

TABLE 3.2 Nissan's contribution, approach and indicators for SDGs 12 and 13

SDG goal target	Nissan's contribution	Nissan's approach	Indicators	FY2017 results	Targets
12.4	Reducing air pollutants	Reducing air pollutants from the manufacturing process.	VOC emissions NOx emissions SOx emissions	11,152 tonnes 651 tonnes 36 tonnes	–
12.5	Reducing waste	Incorporate the three Rs at the car design stage and reduce waste materials. Reduce waste materials from the manufacturing process with methods, such as recycling.	End-of-life vehicle recovery rate (Japan) Waste reduction rate (Business as Usual ratio)	99.7% 10.5%	– Global: 1%/year
12.6	Providing information about sustainability	Provide stakeholders with information through a sustainability report and other media.	–	–	–
13.1	Reducing greenhouse gas emissions	Reduce CO_2 emissions from new cars. Reduce CO_2 emissions from corporate activities. Use carbon credits and reduce CO_2 emissions.	CO_2 emission reduction from new cars (vs. FY2000) CO_2 emission reduction per vehicle sold (vs. FY2005) Credit amount (Spain)	33.4% 29.2% reduction. 45,477t- CO_2	Reduce CO_2 emissions by 40% relative to 2000 levels by FY2022 Reduce CO_2 emissions by 30% relative to 2005 levels by FY2022 –

Source: Based on Nissan, 2018, para. 3.

accident injuries and deaths (SDG3) and to promote sustainable community building and improved mobility (SDG11).

(p. 21)

The report also records that Toyota's implementation framework for sustainable development includes the Corporate Planning Meeting and the Corporate Governance Meeting, which carry out their respective activities from a long-term, company-wide perspective. BMW (2017) identified SDGs 11, 12 and 13 "as areas in which we can have the greatest potential impact" (p. 16), whilst Audi (2017a) was equally specific, noting that "with our comprehensive measures for involving our employees in the digitalization process, Audi is contributing toward the goals to 'Ensure inclusive and equitable quality education for all and promote lifelong learning' (SDG4) and 'Decent work and economic growth' (SDG8)" (para.7). Additionally, "with our measures at the Audi plant in Brussels, we are contributing toward the goals 'Ensuring sustainable consumption and production patterns' (SDG 12) and 'Take urgent action to combat climate change and its impacts' (SDG13)" (Audi, 2017b, para.8). Daimler (2018) took the view that "although the SDGs are directed primarily at governments and countries, the achievement of these goals will depend greatly on businesses because of their innovative spirit and extensive ability to make investments," and identified SDGs 8, 9, 11, 12 and 13, which "are greatly influenced by our business model and value chain and where we can actually bring about change" (para.8).

Actions and activities regarding specific SDGs

In addition to the comprehensive approach taken by Nissan, noted earlier, more detail is provided by other automobile companies and associated reports regarding actions and activities relating to specific SDGs. As regards SDG3, for example, Ford (Ford Motor Company, 2018) notes,

Health and safety is our number one priority. We are committed to ensuring the safety and well-being of our people in our facilities around the world, those in our extensive supply chain and when our customers get behind the wheel.

(para. 5)

Volvo (Volvo Group, 2018) notes "the target to halve the number of global deaths and injuries from road traffic accidents by 2020" as being of particular importance and gave as examples of their activities "safety focus in product development; safety features in our vehicles and machines; safety training for drivers and operators and for school children, cyclists and other road users" (para.4). Similarly, Jaguar Land Rover's Advanced Research Centre is working on a suit of groundbreaking new technologies that aim to prevent future road accidents. In a developing world context, Tata Motors set up commercial vehicle driving centres in partnership with public institutes to promote road safety issues in India, where the company "provides training content, advises aspiring agencies on establishing and running driver training schools, monitors the quality of training, and assists in networking with potential employers for trainees" (United Nations & KPMG, 2017, p. 17). Hyundai Motors worked in partnership with a public health non-profit organisation to provide mobile medical vehicles and service access in a number of developing countries including Ethiopia, Nigeria, Ghana and Rwanda. "These vehicles are designed to allow doctors to perform basic internal medical examinations for those who lack access to healthcare facilities. A mobile health-clinic vehicle is increasingly recognized as a valuable alternative for health-care services to vulnerable populations" (United Nations & KPMG, 2017, p. 17).

SDG4 is supported by Fiat Chrysler and Audi, but in addition Jaguar Land Rover's "Inspiring Tomorrow's Engineers" programme "promotes learning and engagement in STEM subjects in collaboration with schools and colleges to inspire young people to consider engineering and manufacturing careers." Over 2.5 million young people have participated in the programme, which has provided pupils in 11 countries with hands-on projects that enable them to explore different aspects of the automotive industry in a stimulating and exciting way. In addition to raising awareness about engineering and automotive technologies, "the projects also help young people develop communication, team-work, project management and ICT skills" (United Nations & KPMG, 2017, p. 19). To this end, cybersecurity, autonomous car and coding challenges were introduced into the company's national and global education challenges in 2017 to "help students develop technical skills and emphasise the importance of software innovation in developing clean, safe and smart cutting edge technologies" (Society of Motor Manufacturers and Traders, 2018, p. 7). In a similar vein, Volvo Group, together with the US Agency for International Development and the Swedish International Development Cooperation Agency, entered into a partnership to provide vocational training schools for 4,500 young people in ten countries between 2013 and 2018, primarily in Africa and South-East Asia.

For SDG6, Ford maintains that "water is also critical to our manufacturing operations so we continually strive to reduce our water consumption, as well as that of our supply chain" (Ford Motor Company, 2018, para.10). By cutting the water used in everything from cooling towers to washing parts to paint operations, the company had already reduced its total global water use by 62% between 2000 and 2014 and has invested in a range of water-reduction technologies and process improvements. These include "membrane biological reactors and reverse-osmosis processes to recycle water from on-site wastewater treatment plants in more arid regions" and "Minimum Quantity Lubrication which uses a 'dry-machining' process to lubricate cutting tools with a very small amount of oil" (United Nations & KPMG, 2017, p. 24). General Motors (2017b) similarly note that the company

is committed to finding ways to not only reduce water used in our operations, but to extend the benefits of more efficient processes to others. For example, we recently finished our first full year reusing stormwater for process water at the Detroit Hamtramck Assembly plant. The savings equate to nearly $2 million per year for GM. The savings also benefit the city of Detroit: by creating a pond to collect stormwater, we reduce stormwater discharge. Some of the collected water is sent to Detroit Renewable Power, where it is turned into steam that heats and cools the assembly plant and 145 other Detroit businesses. GM is looking to replicate this concept at other sites with similar environmental conditions.

(para. 1)

Another example here is the "zero discharge" policy introduced by Daimler in its new plant in Chennai in southern India, where all water is recycled through a system of pipes, pumps, filters, and evaporators.

Regarding SDG9, Volvo (Volvo Group, 2018) put "particular emphasis on the targets to develop quality, reliable, sustainable and resilient infrastructure including

TABLE 3.3 FCA's material sustainability topics mapped against SDGs

FCA's Material Sustainability Topics	Good Health and Well-being	Quality Education	Gender Equality	Clean Water and Sanitation	Affordable and Clean Energy	Decent Work and Economic Growth	Industry, Innovation and Infrastructure	Reduced Inequalities	Sustainable Cities and Communities	Responsible Consumption and Production	Climate Action
Business integrity			▓			▓		▓			▓
Vehicle safety	▓						▓		▓		
Vehicle quality							▓				
Customer satisfaction											
Research and innovation					▓		▓		▓		▓
Vehicle fuel economy							▓		▓	▓	▓
Vehicle CO₂ emissions							▓		▓	▓	▓
Hybrid, electric systems					▓				▓		▓
Employee health and safety	▓										
Employee well-being and work-life balance	▓		▓			▓					
Renewable energy					▓					▓	▓
Water consumption				▓			▓			▓	
Energy consumption					▓		▓			▓	▓
Risk management											▓
Human rights			▓			▓		▓			
Alternative fuels					▓				▓	▓	▓
Alternative mobility solutions							▓		▓		▓
Employee diversity and equal opportunity			▓			▓		▓			
Employee development		▓	▓			▓		▓			
Biodiversity conservation										▓	
Recycled and recyclable materials										▓	
Waste management							▓			▓	
Emissions from operations							▓		▓	▓	▓
Engagement with business partners						▓	▓			▓	▓
Raw materials sourcing										▓	
Community engagement		▓	▓			▓	▓	▓	▓		
Emissions from logistics									▓	▓	▓

Source: Fiat Chrysler Automobiles, 2018, p. 13.

development in developing countries through enhanced financial, technological and technical support to African countries" and gave as examples of their commitment to "efficient and reliable trucks and machines in the construction segment; investments in innovative technologies such as automation, electromobility and connectivity for construction sites; (and) vocational schools in Africa" (para.6). Ford concludes,

> Today's transportation networks are congested and inefficient, especially in urban areas. But we have an alternative vision of mobility in the future: an integrated system that employs advanced technologies, shared mobility services and autonomous vehicle technology to help people move more safely, confidently and freely.
>
> *(Ford Motor Company, 2018, para.14)*

The company is "developing alternative fuels and powertrain technology with improved fuel economy and lower emissions, including significant investments in electrified vehicle technology" (para.15).

Of the companies surveyed, only Fiat Chrysler and General Motors explicitly support SDG10. GM has set up a range of "Employee Resource Groups," each with its own business plan, to engage in local communities, plan talent acquisition and provide business support, whilst at the same time helping the company to better understand consumer markets (United Nations & KPMG, 2017, p. 31). There have been other relevant examples from the industry in recent decades. Ford, for example, established a supplier diversity development programme in the 1970s to support minority and women-owned businesses and develop the profitability of a diverse range of suppliers.

As regards SDG11, BMW (2017) claims that

> with our integrated mobility services and innovative approaches, we want to change mobility patterns in selected metropolitan areas in a sustainable way. These include our car-sharing services DriveNow and ReachNow, which increasingly offer electric vehicles, as well as the electric scooter specially designed for commuter traffic in cities." (p.16)

In 2015, the company created an "Urban Mobility Competence Centre (UMCC)," which "supports the paradigm shift from cities suitable for cars to cities suitable for people." The UMCC supports the work of BMW with cities and other partners to develop new concepts for future urban mobility and improve city living conditions. The company also has a special investment fund (BMW i Ventures) for early stage companies with promising mobility concepts and claims that "with competitions and internal start-up programmes, we promote the development of further innovation in the context of SDG11 in a targeted manner" (p. 16).

In a similar vein, Ford (Ford Motor Company, 2018) claims, "Our mobility services and solutions will help the cities of tomorrow address a host of challenges. These range from traffic congestion to poor air quality" (para.18) and that "our research and development of global mobility solutions and services, from self-driving vehicles to the technology needed for smart cities, will give people greater freedom of movement in the future" (para.19). The company also highlights its role in "Project Better World," which "is rooted in Ford's belief in social business – being intentional about the business of making the world a better place." This project provides the framework for Ford to work with "government agencies, corporations, civil society, impact investors, social entrepreneurs and academia to find ways to improve the human condition" (para.20). Activities focus on the key areas of health, education and driver safety to date in three main locations: India, Nigeria and South Africa. Working with four major partners – World Vision, Riders for Health, George Washington University and Global Water Challenge – "our activities have positively impacted 140,000 lives to date." These include, for example, provision of mobile clinics and libraries, water, sanitation and hygiene training and vaccination programmes where Ford vehicles have been deployed to deliver these services. Again, in the context of SDG11, Volvo identified the specific target to provide access to safe, affordable, accessible and sustainable transport systems for all by 2020, as one they could promote and support. They noted as examples of their activities "electriCity and increased fleet of hybrid buses" with the assertion that "both Volvo Trucks and Renault Trucks will start selling electric trucks in 2019" (Volvo Group, 2017, p. 63), and General Motors has introduced a car-sharing scheme (Maven) as an alternative to car ownership. It is customised to both rural and city environments and is priced in a simple manner to include insurance and fuel (United Nations & KPMG, 2017, p. 33).

Regarding SDG12, Ford are undertaking a number of measures, including

> directly managing the impacts of operations by lowering energy consumption and reducing emissions from our manufacturing and logistics, as well as responsible water stewardship and waste reduction; efficient resource use, including the use of recycled, renewable and sustainable materials; helping reduce the environmental impacts of our key suppliers; and conducting due diligence to ensure the responsible sourcing of raw materials in compliance with local laws, reporting frameworks and respect for indigenous populations.
> *(Ford Motor Company, 2018, para.23)*

In this context, Bentley Motors has become the first UK car manufacturer to achieve the ISO 14001 (2015) Environmental Management Standard, which assesses organisations against a broader set of their environmental policies compared with the original 1999 14001 standard. At Bentley's Crewe HQ, the roof-mounted solar panels contribute up to 40% of the site's electricity requirements, reducing CO_2 levels by over 2,500 tonnes a year. The company is also constructing the largest solar car port in the United Kingdom. BMW (2017) states, "We continuously reduce CO_2 emissions and resource usage per vehicle produced. In our locations worldwide, we are increasingly focusing on renewable energy and are also working with our supplier network towards improving resource efficiency" (p. 16). The company also founded a joint venture (Digital Energy Solutions) in 2015 to provide digital-based services to subject matter experts and harness the potential of renewable energy; a further joint venture (Encory) was founded in 2016 to promote the recycling of vehicle parts.

SDG13 was the only SDG explicitly supported by all companies surveyed. Volvo (Volvo Group, 2018), for example, cites as examples of their activities: "Fuel efficiency and alternative fuel focus in product development; activities to lower energy consumption and reduce emissions from operations; commitments and action towards emissions and energy efficiency through the WWF Climate Savers program" (para.10). BMW (2017) asserts,

> We are continuously reducing the CO_2 emissions of our vehicle fleet . . . we expect emissions to further decrease in the long run. Electromobility is an essential component of our CO_2 strategy. We are consistently increasing the proportion of electrified drive systems in our model range and therefore not only make a contribution towards the reduction of greenhouse gas emissions, but also towards improved air quality in urban areas.
>
> *(p. 16)*

Hyundai has set up a taskforce to oversee climate change activities, including the achievement of greenhouse gas reduction goals, and to facilitate any necessary investments. The company is taking a range of steps to "develop ecofriendly cars and reduce the amount of greenhouse gases created during the manufacturing of vehicles" (United Nations & KPMG, 2017, p. 37). Ford is pursuing a "comprehensive climate change strategy" that "focuses on reducing vehicle emissions, eco-efficient operations with lower greenhouse gas emissions and reduced energy consumption at our facilities, and helping our suppliers reduce their environmental impacts." In addition, the company has electrification plans that are "focused on delivering affordable electric vehicles at scale, to reduce the emissions associated with the use of our vehicles," and Ford is "using sustainable materials to lower greenhouse gas emissions and energy use, and move away from plastics made from fossil fuels" (Ford Motor Company, 2018, paras.26–29).

By contrast, with the exception of Nissan, none of the companies expressed any specific support for, or contribution to, SDGs 1, 2, 14, 15 or 17, although Ford claimed to "contribute to many of the other SDGs, illustrating the significant role that transportation and the freedom to move plays in increasing social mobility and driving human progress" (Ford Motor Company, 2018, para.30). However, in the context of SDG15, Jaguar Land Rover has introduced ecology strategies for all its sites, with a view to enhancing biodiversity. An example here is at the company's UK Engine Manufacturing Centre, where it has created an "ecological corridor for wildlife," stretching across the site to encourage the natural movement of species. Bat boxes, insect houses and dead wood stumps have been installed to attract bats, birds, small mammals, invertebrates and amphibians to the site. Similarly, Toyota have created an "Eco HQ" in Burgh Heath, Surrey, where they have created a series of special garden areas to increase biodiversity and attract wildlife to thrive. These areas also accommodate a series of areas for staff relaxation and leisure and provide the offices with an attractive outdoor environment.

Discussion

The automotive industry in general has been very keen to emphasise its commitment to the SDGs and has in many instances incorporated these into its business and sustainability strategies and reporting. Nearly all of the companies reviewed were specific in supporting particular SDGs, with only Volkswagen (the parent company of Audi) not following this trend. The *Volkswagen Annual Report* (Volkswagen, 2017) notes, "The Volkswagen Group is committed to sustainable, transparent and responsible corporate governance," but points out that "the complexity of our Company, with its twelve brands, more than 642 thousand employees and 120 production locations" is "the biggest challenge we face in implementing this at all levels and at every step in the value chain" (para.1). Overall, however, the picture is one of commitment to the SDGs and a realisation of the key role that the automotive industry can play in their achievement. A number of issues emerge that are worthy of discussion.

First, the degree of radical change that the industry will be experiencing in the period up to 2030 and the relevance of this change to the SDGs sets the automobile industry apart from many other industry sectors. Its core products – motor vehicles powered by petroleum or diesel engines – are being transformed in terms of engine efficiency, electrification and automated driving. This puts the industry in a key position to contribute to a wide range of the SDGs.

Second, the concept of shared value is evident in many of the company reports. Volvo, for example, notes, "Creating shared value involves moving both our business and society forward. We enhance our competitiveness while simultaneously advancing the economic, environmental and social conditions of the societies in which we operate." The company adds, "The highest potential for mutual benefit is where our business significantly interacts with society. Therefore, our selected focus areas are: education and skills development, traffic and worksite safety and environmental sustainability" (Volvo Group, 2017, p. 78).

Third, the role of stakeholders and partners is seen as of critical importance. Ford (Ford Motor Company, 2018) notes, "Such global challenges require effective, multi-stakeholder collaboration at a local, national and international level. So as we strive to meet these ambitions, we also call on all our stakeholders and partners to join us in our efforts" (para.3). Similarly, Honda (2018) states,

> Key issues to be addressed are organized from our perspective and from the viewpoint of our stakeholders . . . this resulted in the successful visualization of critical issues on a priority basis as a mobility company, including the realization of a carbon-free and collision-free mobile society.
>
> *(p. 16)*

As regards emissions reduction, the industry body concludes,

> The industry recognises its role in reducing total emissions from the fleet, but vehicle use, driving style, traffic flow and congestion, weather and other

variables can influence performance. Therefore, ongoing and collective action is required from all stakeholders to deliver the necessary emissions reductions.
(Society of Motor Manufacturers and Traders, 2018, p. 18)

Fourth, the incorporation of the SDGs into corporate governance is apparent in many of the companies studied. For example, Hyundai's Business Strategy Planning Division has an office dedicated to reporting important climate change issues directly to executive management so that these issues can be reflected in company strategy. Toyota's implementation framework for sustainable development includes the Corporate Planning Meeting and the Corporate Governance Meeting, which now oversee the functions of the company's CSR Committee. The Corporate Planning Meeting, under the Shareholders' Meeting and Board of Directors, takes a wide range of social issues into account when considering growth and business strategy. "Toyota works to ensure compliance, carry out social contribution activities and address environmental problems" (Toyota, 2017, p. 21). Assessing progress against the SDGs is now an integral part of CSR reporting, as evidenced in particular by Nissan's annual reporting against specific indicators (Table 3.2).

These issues are borne out in the latest sustainability report from the Society of Motor Manufacturers and Traders (2018), which has seen a further increase in the number of signatories and for the first time includes a materiality assessment (Figure 3.1), which outlines the key areas for the industry and external stakeholders,

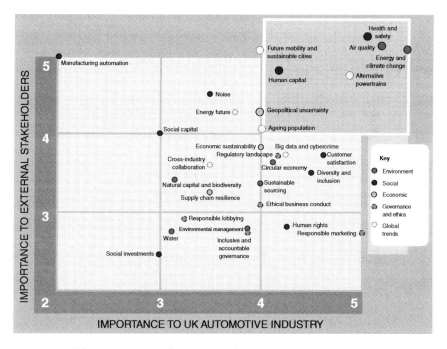

FIGURE 3.1 The automotive industry materiality assessment

Source: Society of Motor Manufacturers and Traders, 2018, p. 30.

examining current, emerging and future priorities of vehicle manufacturers and suppliers, as well as other stakeholders, including government advisors, academics, charities, environmental NGOs and trade unions. The majority of issues identified as being of high importance to the automotive industry and to external stakeholders align with one or other of the SDGs.

Conclusion

The majority of the leading automobile companies have fully embraced the SDGs and the role the industry can play in their realisation. The recent sustainability report from the industry body (Society of Motor Manufacturers and Traders, 2018) suggests that

> the automotive industry welcomes the SDGs and is committed to supporting the actions formulated within them as part of its sustainability strategy, with a focus on its value chain. We believe that companies, governments and other organisations can make a positive contribution towards the attainment of the SDGs.
>
> *(p. 6)*

This emphasis on collective and coordinated action is a recurrent theme in much of the literature, and it is clear that the industry is keen to involve and work with other entities in promoting and adhering to the SDGs and achieving their goals well beyond the associated indicators. In 2001, Liikanen (2001) suggested that the future presented "a suite of great challenges to be met, in increasing the sustainability of the motor industry, both within the EU and on a global basis" (p. 4). More recently, Tovey (2019) has commented that "the growth of electric vehicles and technology such as self-driving systems means the sector will see more change in the next few years than in the previous 100" (p. 3). Within this context of radical change in the industry, there is no doubt that automobile companies can make a major contribution to the attainment of the SDGs, both in the developed and developing worlds, but major challenges remain that will require the involvement and commitment of other parties if they are to be successfully met.

References

Audi. (2017a). *Thinking outside the box*. Retrieved October 24, 2018, from www.audi.com/en/company/sustainability/digital-revolution.html

Audi. (2017b). *Thinking outside the box*. Retrieved October 30, 2018, from www.audi.com/en/experience-audi/mobility-and-trends/working-world/digital-revolution.html

BMW. (2017). *Sustainability value report 2017*. Retrieved October 24, 2018, from www.bmwgroup.com/content/dam/bmw-group-websites/bmwgroup_com/ir/downloads/en/2017/BMW-Group-SustainableValueReport-2017-EN.pdf

Daimler. (2018). *Sustainability strategy and sustainable development goals*. Retrieved June 19, 2019, from www.daimler.com/sustainability/strategie.html

Fiat Chrysler Automobiles Group. (2017). *Fiat Chrysler automobiles releases 2017 sustainability report*. Retrieved October 16, 2018, from www.fcagroup.com/en-US/sustainability/fca_news/Pages/Fiat_Chrysler_Automobiles_releases_2017_Sustainability_Report.aspx

Fiat Chrysler Automobiles Group. (2018). *2018 sustainability report*. Retrieved June 21, 2019, from www.fcagroup.com/en-US/investors/financial_information_reports/sustainability_reports/sustainability_reports/FCA_2018_Sustainability_Report.pdf

Ford Motor Company. (2018). *Sustainability report 2017/18 – contributing to the UN SDGs*. Retrieved October 18, 2018, from https://corporate.ford.com/microsites/sustainability-report-2017-18/strategy-governance/sdg.html

General Motors. (2017a). *General motors 2017 sustainability report: UN sustainable development goals*. Retrieved May 21, 2019, from www.gmsustainability.com/unsdg.html

General Motors. (2017b). *General motors 2017 sustainability report: Operations*. Retrieved May 21, 2019, from www.gmsustainability.com/act/operations/water.html

Honda. (2018). *Sustainability report 2018*. Retrieved October 27, 2018, from https://global.honda/content/dam/site/global/about/cq_img/sustainability/report/pdf/2018/Honda-SR-2018-en-all-02.pdf

Liikanen, E. (2001, November 21). *Sustainability in the car industry: Speech to the UK motor industry reception*. Brussels. European Commission, Enterprise and Information Society. Retrieved November 7, 2018, from europa.eu/rapid/press-release_SPEECH-01-579_en.pdf

National Instruments. (2018). *Automotive research user handbook: Prototypes and testbeds to validate the transportation solutions of tomorrow*. National Instruments, IEEE.

Nissan. (2018). *Sustainability report 2018*. Retrieved October 28, 2018, from www.nissan-global.com/EN/SUSTAINABILITY/REPORT/

SMMT News. (2017). *UK Automotive achieves record turnover of £77.5 billion, marking seventh consecutive year of growth*. Retrieved November 5, 2018, from www.smmt.co.uk/2017/06/uk-automotive-achieves-record-turnover-77-5-billion-marking-seventh-consecutive-year-growth/

Society of Motor Manufacturers and Traders. (2018). *2018 automotive sustainability report* (19th ed.). Retrieved November 7, 2018, from www.smmt.co.uk/wp-content/uploads/sites/2/SMMT-Sustainability-Report-2018-1.pdf

Tovey, A. (2019, June 7). Will Hackett's hatchet sever Ford's loyalty to UK? *The Daily Telegraph*. Business section, p. 3.

Toyota. (2017). *Toyota annual report 2017*. Retrieved October 27, 2018, from www.toyota-global.com/pages/contents/investors/ir_library/annual/pdf/2017/ar17_4_en.pdf

United Nations and KPMG. (2017). *SDG industry matrix – transportation*. Retrieved November 5, 2018, from https://home.kpmg/content/dam/kpmg/xx/pdf/2017/05/sdg-transportation.pdf

Volkswagen. (2017). *Volkswagen annual report 2017*. Retrieved October 24, 2018, from http://annualreport2017.volkswagenag.com/group-management-report/sustainable-value-enhancement/sustainability.html

Volvo Group. (2017). *Annual and sustainability report 2017*. Retrieved October 29, 2018, from www.volvogroup.com/content/dam/volvo/volvo-group/markets/global/en-en/investors/reports-and-presentations/annual-reports/annual-and-sustainability-report-2017.pdf).

Volvo Group. (2018). *Sustainable development goals*. Retrieved November 5, 2018, from www.volvogroup.com/en-en/about-us/csr-and-sustainability/supporting-development-goals.html

4

THE HOTEL INDUSTRY

Introduction

The United Nations World Tourism Organisation (UNWTO) and United Nations Global Compact Network Spain (2016) have argued that "tourism is one of the most dynamic and far reaching economic sectors, and can make a decisive contribution to the achievement of the SDGs" (p. 28). Further, the UNWTO and the United Nations Development Programme (2017) "are committed to inspiring leadership and facilitating collaboration among all stakeholders to realize the SDGs and targets that are spelled out in the 2030 Agenda for Sustainable Development" (p. 10). At the same time, the International Tourism Partnership (2018a) suggested that the SDGs "send out a clear call to action for the wider industry about the critical importance of using the UN SDGs as a focal point to drive responsible business in hospitality" (para.4). From outside the industry, Jones, Hillier and Comfort (2017) have argued that

> while the tourism and hospitality industry can be seen to have a vital role to play in the drive towards a more sustainable future, the leading players within the industry must address a number of challenges as they look to make a meaningful contribution to the achievement of the SDGs.
>
> *(p. 10)*

The eight hotel groups reviewed in this chapter all feature in the "Top Ten Leading Hotel Groups" (Tourism Review, 2017). As the largest players within the hotel industry, the selected companies might be expected to reflect innovative thinking in their approach to the SDGs. Marriott International, the world's largest hotel group, is a US multinational hospitality company, headquartered in Bethesda, Maryland, and owns some 6,500 properties in over 120 countries. AccorHotels is a French multinational company that owns, manages and franchises hotels, resorts and vacation properties and operates over 4,000 hotels in 100 countries. The Wyndham Hotels and Resort is the world's largest hotel franchise company and trades as a number of brands, including Wyndham, Ramada and Days Inn, in over 70 countries. Hilton is a major US-based hospitality company and either owns, manages or franchises over 570 hotels and resorts in 85 countries. The Hyatt Hotel Corporation is headquartered in Chicago, Illinois, and manages and franchises over 700 hotels, resorts and vacation properties in some 50 countries. Meliá Hotels International, a Spanish-based hotel chain, is the market leader in resort and urban hotels within Spain and operates 375 hotels in 40 other countries. InterContinental Hotel Group (IHG®) is a UK-based multinational hospitality group and operates more than 5,600 hotels in over 100 countries. The final hotel group, the NH Hotel group, is a Spanish-based hotel chain and has some 375 hotels in 29 countries, principally in Europe and Latin America. In addition, two hotel organisations are included in the review. The International Tourism Partnership (ITP) is a worldwide organisation comprising some of the world's largest hotel companies focusing on improved sustainability, and the UNWTO is the agency responsible for the promotion of responsible, sustainable and universally accessible tourism. As the leading international organisation in the field of tourism, UNWTO "promotes tourism as a driver of economic growth, inclusive development and environmental sustainability, and offers leadership and support to the sector in advancing knowledge and tourism policies worldwide" (United Nations World Tourism Organization, 2018a, para.2).

Overview of the hotel industry and the SDGs

The selected hotel companies have addressed the SDGs in a variety of ways. Some of the companies referenced specific SDGs, whilst others stressed their own sustainability practices that could be seen as being in support of some of the SDGs (Table 4.1). IHG noted "the SDGs are wide ranging and we have identified the seven where we believe that, in partnership with our owners, colleagues and wider stakeholder community, IHG can make the greatest impact" (Green Hotelier, 2017, para.4). More specifically, IHG targeted seven of the SDGs, namely SDGs 6, 8, 10, 11, 12, 13 and 17 in line with the company's "responsible business approach across the hotel life-cycle" (Figure 4.1).

Hilton (2017) reported that the company had properties in over 100 countries and that the company was looking "to harness our global hospitality mission to help drive local solutions in the communities, where we operate, aligning our action to the SDGs" (p. 17). Hilton addressed all 17 of the SDGs by aligning each of them to specific targets. The company notes, for example, "another way we seek to incorporate the SDGs in our work is by framing our programmatic areas to align directly with the targets and indicators for specific SDGs. Our Safe Water Strategic Initiative, for example, is directly aligned with SDG 6: Clean Water Sanitation" (Hilton, 2018a, para.11). In his "Executive Statement" for Hilton's 2017 CSR Report, Christopher J. Nasetta, President and Chief Executive Officer, suggested "at Hilton, we're more and more inspired every day to use our hospitality for good and as a truly global company, we are serious about our role in helping the international community reach the UN SDGs" (Hilton, 2017, p. 2).

The Hyatt Hotel Corporation (2018) noted "our corporate responsibility work supports the mission of the UN SDGs" (para.5). The company's corporate responsibility strategy embraces six key sets of issues, namely, "our people," "our communities," "human rights," "our planet," "responsible sourcing" and "responsible seafood"; each of these sets of issues is aligned to a number of the SDGs (para.2). Hyatt's commitment to "our people", for example, is aligned to SDGs 5, 8 and 10, the company's commitment to "our planet" is aligned to SDGs 6, 7, 12 and 13 and the commitment to responsible sourcing is aligned to SDGs 8, 12, 14 and 15. Similarly, Wyndham Hotels and Resorts (2018) aligned its material CSR goals to ten of the SDGs, namely SDGs 1, 2, 3 4, 5, 6, 8, 13, 15 and 17.

In 2018, Marriott International (2017) launched "Serve 360," which the company claimed was "guided by the UN SDGs" (para.3). Ray Bennett, Chief Global Officer, Global Operations at Marriott International, argued, "as the global hospitality leader with properties and associates across 125 countries and territories, Marriott International has a global responsibility and unique opportunity to be a force for good – from helping to reduce carbon and water use to providing our associates with human trafficking awareness training" (Marriott International, 2017, para.2). Four "priority areas" are identified, these being "advancing the resiliency and development of our communities"; "reducing the company's environmental impacts, sourcing responsibly and operating sustainable hotels"; "helping people prepare for jobs in the hospitality industry"; and "creating a safe and welcoming world for associates and travellers alike" (para.4). These can be seen to broadly accord with SDGs 3, 8, 10, 11, 12 and 13.

In addressing reducing environmental impacts, for example, the company is looking to

> minimize our environmental footprint by sustainably managing our energy and water use, reducing our waste and carbon emissions and increasing the use of renewable energy. We employ innovative technologies to plan, implement, track and communicate how we operate responsibly to mitigate climate-related risk, benefiting our business and the communities in which we operate.
>
> *(Marriott International, 2018, para.2)*

More specifically the company have committed to reducing water use by 15%, carbon emissions by 30% waste by 45% and food waste by 50%, all by 2025, to train all associates to recognise the signs of human trafficking and to embed human rights criteria in recruitment and sourcing policies.

In a similar vein, AccorHotels (2016a) reported looking to contribute to the SDGs through its "Planet 21" sustainable development programme. The company listed key achievements from the programme under four headings, namely,

TABLE 4.1 SDGs addressed by hotel groups and organisations

SDG/ hotel group	Hilton	Marriott	Accor	NH Hotels	Wyndham	Hyatt	ITP	UNWTO	Meliá	IHG
1	x			x						
2	x			x						
3	x	x	x	x					x	
4	x			x		x				
5	x			x	x				x	
6	x			x	x	x				x
7	x					x				
8	x	x	x	x	x	x	x	x	x	x
9	x		x							
10	x	x	x			x	x		x	x
11	x	x	x							x
12	x	x	x	x		x		x	x	x
13	x	x	x	x	x	x	x		x	x
14	x		x			x		x		
15	x		x	x	x					
16	x		x						x	
17	x		x	x			x			x

planting for the planet, the fight against the sexual exploitation of children, eco-design and sustainable food. In evidencing the first of these achievements, the company reported, "at AccorHotels, we ask our customers to reuse their towels. Savings made on water and energy are used to fund tree planting. One tree is planted every minute" (para.5). In promoting healthy and sustainable food, AccorHotels reported its commitment to "offering healthy, balanced and high quality food" including "local products" and "products grown in our kitchen gardens" as well as "reducing food waste" and "banning the use of overfished species in our restaurants" (para. 8). The company notes "we believe that it is our duty to help spread knowledge and promote the progress of all stakeholders in the hotel industry – both businesses and guests. With this collaborative approach to sustainable innovation in mind, we launched Planet 21 Research, a platform for sharing knowledge about sustainable development in the hotel industry" (AccorHotels, 2016b, para.1).

An examination of the company's socio-economic footprint in 2016 revealed that AccorHotels supported "880,000 jobs and mainly creates wealth in our host countries" (AccorHotels, 2016b, para.3). A study of the environmental footprint of AccorHotels (para.4), conducted in 2011, covered the entire life cycle of the

1. Design and development
IHG branded hotels are designed and developed in innovative and responsible ways to be at the heart of their communities.

2. Procurement
We aim to source goods and services in a responsible way. As our franchised and managed hotels are owned by independent third-party owners, these hotels are typically responsible for managing their own independent supply chains. In certain cases, IHG provides a centralised procurement option for hotels.

3. Operations
Our hotels are operated to manage environmental impacts and enhance positive impact on the local economy and local people, whilst also focusing on the safety and security of colleagues and guests.

4. Marketing
We enhance the reputation of IHG and its brands by delivering responsible hotels our guests want.

5. Sales and distribution
We manage key relationships in the business-to-business, transient, leisure, and speciality markets to attract guests to our hotels who value responsible business practices.

6. Renewal
Hotels renew, recycle and reuse materials wherever possible.

IHG responsible business approach across the hotel lifecycle

FIGURE 4.1   IHG's responsible business approach across the hotel life cycle

Source: IHG, 2018, p. 11.

company's activities. This study revealed that the five major environmental impacts were energy consumption, water consumption, waste production, climate change and water eutrophication. The company used the study to encourage, educate and empower its employees to initiate new ideas that reduce its environmental impacts. The Planet 21 strategic themes and related initiatives align with many of the SDGs, notably SDGs 8–15. More specifically, in 2018, the company noted that Planet 21 "establishes commitments for 2016–2020 across the six focus areas of guests, partners, people, communities, food and buildings" and identified SDGs 2, 7, 8, 12 and 16 as being of critical importance for the hotel industry as a whole (AccorHotels, 2018, p. 14).

Meliá Hotels International published its "Global Corporate Social Responsibility Model" in 2015. The company notes

> the SDGs aim, among other things, to end extreme poverty, combat inequality and injustice, and tackle climate change. As a market-leading company, Meliá felt that it should step forward and make the promotion of these SDGs an essential part of its own strategy. In 2015 Meliá matched the SDGs with

the goals of its own CSR model to align Company goals with the universal goals inspired by the United Nations.

(Meliá Hotels International, 2016, para. 5)

The company's CSR model is based around six key principles, namely "human rights and childhood," "employability," "local development and the fight against climate change," "university and knowledge sharing," "culture" and "leadership and reputation" (Meliá Hotels International, 2016, para.2).

More specifically, the hotel group noted that "by integrating the SDGs into its Global CSR Model, Meliá aims to reinforce its own approach to:

- Ensure a consistent management model that seeks continuous improvement
- Promote a model of responsible management in the value chain
- Contribute to the generation of social and economic value
- Maintain a proactive attitude in the identification, prevention and mitigation of risks
- Make the fight against climate change a key objective in hotel management
- Strengthen long-term relationships based on trust, respect and transparency

(para. 8)

The company concluded "this is how Meliá is working towards moving towards a sustainable future from a responsible present" (para.9). Overall, although not explicitly stated, there is some correlation between, on the one hand, the company's CSR model, its principles and approach and, on the other, several of the SDGs, notably 3, 5, 8, 10, 12, 13 and 16.

The NH Hotels Group claimed that the SDGs had been used along with other "criteria," including the ten principles of the UN Global Reporting Compact and the G4 guidelines of the Global Reporting Initiative for Sustainability Reporting, to prepare its *2017 Annual Report* (NH Hotels Group, 2018, para.7). Here, the focus is on the SDGs in which NH Hotel Group has a direct impact. This builds upon their earlier statement that "the company has identified the SDGs with the most direct impact on its daily activities. These include Goals 3 (Good Health & Wellbeing), 8 (Decent Work & Economic Growth), 12 (Responsible Consumption & Production), 13 (Climate Change), 16 (Peace, Justice & Strong Institutions) and 17 (Partnerships)" (NH Hotels Group, 2016, p. 41).

The ITP is "a global sector-led organisation, bringing together the world's most powerful hotel companies in an alliance focused on a single ambition: to lead the industry through example with clear and quantifiable commitments to improved sustainability" (International Tourism Partnership, 2018a, para.13). The organisation notes its belief that "the hotel industry can be a force for good and make a positive contribution to the United Nations' Sustainable Development Goals and to the COP 21 climate agreements. By working together, we can drive change further and faster than on our own. Our vision for 2030 is for sustainable growth and a fairer future for all" (ITP, 2018b, paras.1–2) The organisation notes "the critical importance of using the United Nations' SDGs – also called the Global Goals – as a focal point to drive responsible business in hospitality" (para.3). ITP identifies SDGs 4, 6, 8, 10 and 13 as those that align with their own goals where the hotel industry can make a particular impact (Figure 4.1). In addition, however, as noted by Emily McLeish, Senior Brand and Marketing Communications Manager,

> our work also closely aligns to SDG17. We bring together the leading hotels from around the world to work collaboratively on issues affecting society and the environment. We also use the strength of this network to initiate cross-sector collaboration – working with governments or other industry bodies where we have shared aims – such as tackling modern slavery in the value chain.
>
> *(E. McLeish, personal communication, May 30, 2019)*

Youth Employment: To collectively impact one million young people through employability programmes by 2030, thereby doubling our current impact on youth unemployment. (SDGs 4 and 8)

Water: To embed water stewardship programmes to reduce the number of people affected by water scarcity and identify ways to address water scarcity. (SDG6)

Carbon: To embrace science-based targets and encourage the wider industry to join in reducing emissions at scale. (SDG13)

Human Rights: To raise awareness of human rights risks, embed human rights into corporate governance and address risks arising in the labour supply chain and during construction. (SDGs 8 and 10)

FIGURE 4.2 International Tourism Partnership: our goals

Source: ITP, 2018b, para. 3.

The UNWTO notes, in reference to the SDGs, that it

> is placing its efforts and tireless work in contributing with its technical assistance and capacity building to the achievement of these global goals. UNWTO is working with governments, public and private partners, development banks, international and regional finance institutions, the UN agencies and international organizations to help achieve the SDGs, placing an emphasis on Goals 8, 12 and 14, in which tourism is featured.
>
> *(United Nations World Tourism Organisation, 2018b, para 2)*

Actions and activities regarding specific SDGs

In addressing SDG1, Hilton's "target alignment" stressed its commitment to "eradicate extreme poverty," "implement social protection systems" and provide "equal rights to economic resources" (Hilton, 2017, p. 17). More specifically, Hilton reported being "committed to opening doors for 1 million young people by 2019 to connecting, preparing or employing them" and being "committed to connecting, preparing or employing refugees in Europe" (Hilton, 2017, p. 17). Further, Hilton reported that as a founding member of the Global Apprenticeship Network, the company had supported over 2,500 apprenticeships and encouraged training legislation in Egypt, Namibia, Saudi Arabia, Turkey, the United Kingdom and the United States.

As regards SDG3, NH Hotels (2016) note

> work is done on three concepts: nutrition, wellbeing and local flavour. That is, responsible consumption and positive impact on health and the social and environmental areas. In this way, the Company is ambassador of a healthy diet and healthy habits, not only for guests, but also for all stakeholders. Evidence: Healthy breakfast offered at 368 hotels in 28 countries and enjoyed by over 6,000,000 customers.
>
> *(p. 41)*

Hilton's target alignment to SDG6 embraced "access to safe drinking water," "adequate sanitation and hygiene" and "water resource management" (Hilton, 2017, p. 18). In evidencing these targets, Hilton reported reducing water consumption by 20% per square foot of hotel space since 2008, signing on for the UN's Chief Executive Officer Water Mandate and launching a number of global water stewardship pilot schemes in high risks regions in the United States, South Africa and China.

SDG8 is one of the three SDGs actively promoted by the United Nations World Trade Organisation (2018b). They note that

> by giving access to decent work opportunities in the tourism sector, society – particularly youth and women – can benefit from enhanced skills and professional development. The sector's contribution to job creation is recognised

in target 8.9 "By 2030, devise and implement policies to promote sustainable tourism that creates jobs and promotes local culture and products."

(para. 6)

This aspiration is supported by NH Hotel Group (2016), which states,

> The capacity to create jobs is one of NH Hotel Group's values. The Company works on a number of initiatives in collaboration with the public sector and third-sector organizations, not only to improve employability and fight against inequality, but also to create opportunities. Evidence: Youth Career Initiative (YCI) is a high impact international initiative for the training and professional development of youth at risk of exclusion, of which NH Hotel Group is a member.
>
> *(p. 41)*

IHG (2018) notes, "Aside from our own business, we also recognise the potential positive impact we can bring to our communities by building skills and education in hospitality," and, more specifically, record that "more than 13,531 people improved their chances of employment through our IHG Academy in 2018, and we also launched a new programme for communities and charitable giving, True Hospitality for Good" (p. 6). Additionally, IHG (2016) claims, in the context of SDG11, that "our hotels provide critical economic stimulation in the communities within which they operate, including in developing countries" and that "we ensure our hotels are prepared and able to play an active role in supporting those impacted by disasters, helping local communities get back on their feet quickly" (p. 9).

For SDG12 and SDG13, NH Hotel Group (2016) comments that they have plans "that specifically promote the achievement of these two Goals" these being the "Green Savings Project: Savings in consumption by the Company (water, energy and other related aspects, such as laundry)" and the "Green Hotel Project: Sustainable actions with customers." The company cites as evidence that "all hotels submit monthly reports on water and energy consumption, as well as carbon footprint. Also, 273 of hotels use green energy sources and 131 have an external environmental certification" (p. 41). Hyatt's (2018) commitment to "our planet" (para.3) includes setting goals to reduce energy and water consumption and greenhouse gas emissions at its hotels, pursuing a variety of waste management and recycling strategies and building a culture of environmental stewardship amongst hotel owners and developers.

Hilton (2017) identified specific target alignments in addressing SDG13 – namely, to improve education and awareness of climate change and to promote mechanisms for climate change-related planning. In addressing these targets, the company reported reducing carbon emissions by 30% per square foot of hotel space and energy consumption by 20% per square foot of hotel space since 2008, activating 1,800 environmental projects in 1,000 communities during Earth Week in 2017. They also claimed to be the first major hospitality brand to have "science-based greenhouse gas targets approved by the Science Based Targets initiative" (p. 19). Additionally, the Conrad N. Hilton Foundation, which funds not-for-profit organisations working to improve the lives of disadvantaged and vulnerable people throughout the world, illustrated some of its work in contributing to the SDGs. On the one hand, the Foundation outlined its belief that philanthropy has an important role to play in supporting the SDGs through "advocacy, facilitating implementation, helping to measure success and in training the next generation of leaders capable of promoting evidence-based solutions that address human development, health and economic and environmental needs at the core of the SDGs" (Hilton Foundation, 2018a, para.6). On the other hand, the Conrad N. Hilton Foundation has argued that "people underestimate the universality of the global goals, assuming they only apply to developing countries," whereas the "we at the Conrad N. Hilton Foundation, firmly understands the relevance of the goals at the domestic level" (Hilton Foundation, 2018b, para.1).

In aligning the company's targets with SDG15, Wyndham Hotels and Resorts (2018) noted the aim was to promote and expand best practices for biodiversity protection across their properties and to partner with suppliers to make a meaningful impact to protect forests. For SDG16, NH Hotel Group (2016) notes,

> Work in relation to this Goal focuses on ethical and effective commitments at all levels. In line with the best ethics and corporate governance practices, a series of rules and principles have been established, which must govern the professional conduct of employees and are intended to involve and engage all stakeholders.

The company cites as evidence "recent updating of the Code of Conduct, training and awareness on the Code of Conduct, and supplier approval policy" (p. 41). The targets for SDG17 for Wyndham Hotels and Resorts (2018) were to continue to advance sustainable development through active participation in industry initiatives with the World Travel and Tourism Council, ITP, Department of Energy and other global partners.

Discussion

A number of issues emerge from the earlier review that merit reflection and discussion. First, the findings reveal marked variation in how the selected leading hotel groups have begun to address the SDGs. One group, Hilton, directly addressed all 17 SDGs, while IHG specifically targeted seven of the SDGs, providing details on how they were approaching each one and performing against their targets (Figure 4.3).

Some of the hotel groups claimed that their corporate sustainability goals and targets had been aligned with the SDGs, whilst others suggested that the SDGs had been a guide for, and/or integrated into, the development of their sustainability strategies. Further, this process of alignment has been pursued in a general rather than a specific manner, and there has been little or no attempt to directly map corporate goals and targets to specific SDGs. Where hotel groups claim to have aligned a relatively small number of key corporate priorities to the SDGs, for example; the link to the specific SDGs can be seen to lack clarity. As such, it will be difficult for the hotel groups that have adopted this alignment or integration approach to assess

Goal	2018 highlights	Our approach
6 CLEAN WATER AND SANITATION	We launched two water stewardship protects in London and Delhi to help us identify key issues where we can develop and apply water innovations that can be replicated in other water stressed locations. In 2018, we achieved a 3.1% reduction in water use per occupied room.	In 2016, we undertook a comprehensive water risk assessment that has helped us identify where to focus our six water stewardship protects.
8 DECENT WORK AND ECONOMIC GROWTH	We offered quality work experience to 13,531 people through our IHG Academy. Our learning and development strategy ensures that we continue to invent in our colleagues, helping them reach their potential whilst delivering an exceptional guest experience.	With tourism generating one in ten jobs globally, we are uniquely positioned to help more people into employment and deliver local economic impact through our entire estate.
10 REDUCED INEQUALITIES	Listed by the Hampton-Alexander Review in the top 10 of companies for female representation across our executive committee and their direct reports. One hundred percent rating in the Human Rights Campaign's Corporate Equality index-making IHG a best place to work for LGBTQ equality for the last four years	Our colleagues represent many cultures, religions, races, sexual orientations and backgrounds and our diversity and inclusion strategy reduces any potential equalities. To help grow our strategy, we launched our Global D&I Board led by our CEO and IHG senior leaders.
11 SUSTAINABLE CITIES AND COMMUNITIES	Our hotels globally implemented 7,825 IHG Green Engage solutions.	Our online sustainability platform the IHG Green Engage system, enables our hotels to operate more sustainably through solutions they can implement in property to report and manage their carbon, energy water and waste. When it comes to our local communities, we work with our hotels to ensure that they are prepared and able to play an active role in the event of a disaster, ensuring our local communities can get back on their feet
12 RESPONSIBLE CONSUMPTION AND PRODUCTION	During 2018, our Procurement and Cost Efficiency (PaCE) team built a responsible procurement team to help drive our responsible business agenda through our supply chain. In partnership with the IHG Owners Association, we launched the Renovation Donation Initiative to reduce the amount of materials reaching landfills and support the important wort of non-profit organisations in the local communities, including workforce development and hospitality skills training programmes.	We have established a Strategic Supplier Management Office (SSMO), which works with out strategic suppliers to maximise realised supplier value and minimise risk through effective supplier relationship management. Through our Greener Stay programme, we reward our loyalty members who defer housekeeping services. Hotels can operate more efficiently by reducing energy and water use, as well as reducing the use of chemicals in the housekeeping process.
13 CLIMATE ACTION	In 2018, we reduced our carbon footprint by 2.2% pet occupied room. Named industry leading for a second consecutive year in the 2018 S&P Dow Jones Sustainability Indices. Our hotels and offices using IHG Green Engage sustainability platform avoided coats of $67 million.	Our online sustainability system IHG Green Engage recommends 200 Green Solutions that help our hotels and offices to reduce thee energy, water and waste.
17 PARTNERSHIPS FOR THE GOALS	Our franchise business model means that working in collaboration with our hotel owners and teams is an essential part of how we embed our approach to responsible business across our hotel estate. Working with the IHG Owners Association we can implement new processes to help our hotels operate in a more sustainable way.	We continue in collaborate with industry associations, NGOs, government and community organisations to embed our programmes and to deliver positive change. Through our longstanding membership of the International Tourism Partnership(ITP), we collaborated with industry peers to develop collective solutions to key sustainability challenges.

FIGURE 4.3 IHG's highlights and approach in support of the SDGs

Source: IHG, 2018, p. 10.

how they are contributing to specific SDGs. On the one hand, such contributions become part of wider corporate contributions to sustainability, and on the other this, approach does not suggest that the majority of the selected hotel groups are "using the UN SDGs as a focal point to drive responsible business in hospitality" (International Tourism Partnership, 2018a, para.12).

Second, and related to the previous point, many of the selected hotel groups' commitments to the SDGs are couched in terms of business imperatives, not least efficiency and continuing growth, as well as sustainability. Ray Bennett, chief global officer, global operations at Marriott International has commented,

> We recognize that how we do business is as important as the business that we do. Incorporating environmental and social initiatives, including human rights awareness training, into our business is not only the right thing to do, it has a direct impact on our profits and beyond.
>
> *(Marriott International, 2017, para.2)*

It is perhaps indicative of this paradox that only three of the hotel groups studied here leant support to SDG14, one of the three SDGs highlighted by UNWTO as being of particular importance for the tourism sector. United Nations World Trade Organisation (2018b) notes,

> Coastal and maritime tourism, tourism's biggest segments . . . rely on healthy marine ecosystems. Tourism development must be a part of integrated Coastal Zone Management in order to help conserve and preserve fragile ecosystems and serve as a vehicle to promote the blue economy.
>
> *(para. 8)*

Third, there are issues concerning the data that is required to measure progress and the processes and procedures that need to be in place to monitor that progress. Regarding SDG12, for example, Target 12.b notes that it is imperative to "develop and implement tools to monitor sustainable development impacts for sustainable tourism which creates jobs, promotes local culture and products." United Nations World Trade Organisation (2018b) recommend the adoption of "sustainable consumption and production (SCP) practices" by the tourism industry, which "can play a significant role in accelerating the global shift towards sustainability." They note that such practices "result in enhanced economic, social and environmental outcomes" (para.7). There was a range of responses to this by the hotel groups studied here, but, encouragingly, several have set clear relevant targets. For example, and as noted earlier, Marriott Hotels has committed to specific measurable reductions in water use, carbon emissions and food waste by 2025. IHG (2018) has developed a "Green Criteria" for suppliers that is now "included with our BSI supplier assessment programme," and the company aims to "increase the percentage of suppliers that meet IHG Green Criteria" (p. 17). The company also reports on water reduction use and on "carbon footprint per occupied room (kgCO$_2$e)" (p. 35), the target for the latter being a reduction of "6–7%" (p. 33) between 2018 and 2020.

Conclusion

A number of trade organisations have argued that tourist industry can play a major role in contributing to the SDGs. The hotel groups studied here have addressed the SDGs in different ways, with the majority aligning the SDGs with their own sustainability objectives and actions or incorporating them in some manner into their existing strategies. IHG and NH Hotels addressed the SDGS more directly, but overall, it is apparent that the hotel industry as a whole has some way to go if it is to play a leading role in contributing to the SDGs. There could be a sharper focus on the SDGs themselves, with a more comprehensive approach to drawing up priorities for the SDGs, whilst addressing the issues of performance measurement in a more systematic manner. Cross-industry bodies, such as the ITP and UNWTO, also have a key role to play in instigating and implementing industry initiatives in support of the SDGs.

References

AccorHotels. (2016a). *With planet 21 AccorHotels Aims to provide a positive hospitality experience*. Retrieved December 7, 2018, from www.accorhotels.com/gb/sustainable-development/index.shtml

AccorHotels. (2016b). *Planet 21 research*. Retrieved June 18, 2018, from www.accorhotels.group/en/commitment/sharing-our-knowledge/planet-21-research

AccorHotels. (2018). *Corporate responsibility report – Australia 2018*. Retrieved June 18, 2018, from https://images.jobsataccor.com.au/wp-content/uploads/AccorHotels-Corporate-Responsibility-Report-2018.pdf

GreenHotelier. (2017). *IHG aligns with SDGs for latest CSR report*. Retrieved May 20, 2019, from www.greenhotelier.org/our-news/industry-news/ihg-aligns-with-sdgs-for-latest-csr-report/

Hilton Foundation. (2017). *Travel with purpose: 2017 CSR report*. Retrieved June 7, 2019, from https://cr.hilton.com/wp-content/uploads/2018/05/Hilton-Corporate-Responsibility-2017.pdf

Hilton Foundation. (2018a). *Sustainable development goals*. Retrieved June 7, 2019, from www.hiltonfoundation.org/sdgs

Hilton Foundation. (2018b). *Making the global, local: How the sustainable development goals can be implemented in the United States*. Retrieved June 18, 2019, from www.hiltonfoundation.org/news/236-making-the-global-local-how-the-sustainable-development-goals-can-be-implemented-in-the-united-states

Hyatt. (2018). *Corporate responsibility at Hyatt*. Retrieved June 14, 2019, from https://about.hyatt.com/en/hyatt-thrive.html

IHG. (2016). *Responsible business report 2016*. Retrieved May 30, 2019, from www.washingtonblade.com/content/files/2017/05/responsible-business-report16.pdf

IHG. (2018). *Responsible business report 2018*. Retrieved May 24, 2019, from www.ihgplc.com/en/responsible-business

International Tourism Partnership. (2018a). *ITP goals for 2030 unite the hotel industry for a sustainable future*. Retrieved May 20, 2019, from www.tourismpartnership.org/global-goals/

International Tourism Partnership. (2018b). *ITP goals for 2030 unite the hotel industry for a sustainable future: Our goals*. Retrieved May 20, 2019, from www.tourismpartnership.org/itp-goals/

Jones, P., Hillier, D., & Comfort, D. (2017). The sustainable development goals and the tourism and hospitality industry. *Athens Journal of Tourism*, 4(1), 7–18.

Marriott International. (2017). *Marriott international unveils global sustainability and social impact commitments to deliver positive change*. Retrieved June 14, 2019, from https://news. marriott.com/2017/11/marriott-international-unveils-global-sustainability-social-impact-commitments-deliver-positive-change/

Marriott International. (2018). *Serve 360 – doing good in every direction*. Retrieved June 14, 2019, from https://serve360.marriott.com/sustain/

Melia Hotels International. (2016). *Integration of sustainable development goals into melia international*. Retrieved May 20, 2019, from www.meliahotelsinternational.com/en/ press-room/11142016/integration-sustainable-development-goals-sdg-melia-hotels-international

NH Hotel Group. (2016). *Annual report 2016: Corporate responsibility report*. Retrieved June 6, 2019, from https://memorianh.com/2016/en/Corporate-Responsibility/files/assets/ common/downloads/Corporate-Responsibility-Report-NH-2016.pdf

NH Hotel Group. (2018). *Annual report: Corporate responsibility report*. Retrieved May 20, 2019, from https://memorianh.com/2018/corporate-responsibility-report/about-the-annual-report-and-corporate-responsibility-report/

Tourism Review. (2017). *Top 10 leading hotel groups*. Retrieved December 8, 2018, from www.tourism-review.com/biggest-hotel-groups-by-revenue-news5501

United Nations World Tourism Organization (UNWTO). (2018a). *Who we are*. Retrieved May 20, 2019, from http://www2.unwto.org/content/who-we-are-0

United Nations World Tourism Organization (UNWTO). (2018b). *Tourism and the SDGs*. Retrieved May 20, 2019, from https://icr.unwto.org/content/tourism-and-sdgs

United Nations World Tourism Organization and United Nations Development Programme. (2017). *Tourism and the sustainable development goals – journey to 2030*. Retrieved June 14, 2019, from www.e-unwto.org/doi/pdf/10.18111/9789284419401

United Nations World Tourism Organisation and United Nations Global Compact Network Spain. (2016). *The tourism sector and the sustainable development goals: Responsible tourism, a global commitment*. Retrieved June 12, 2019, from http://cf.cdn.unwto.org/sites/all/files/ pdf/turismo_responsable_omt_acc.pdf

Wyndham Hotels and Resorts. (2018). *Travelling together for a better world*. Retrieved December 9, 2018, from http://www2.wyndhamdestinations.com/category/corporate-social-responsibility

5

THE MARKETING AND MEDIA INDUSTRIES

Introduction

In June 2016, UN Secretary-General Ban Ki-Moon and six of the world's leading marketing companies launched the "Common Ground" initiative in support of the SDGs, which potentially heralded a new era in which the marketing industry would take a much more active and prominent role in promoting the transition to a more sustainable future. The secretary-general claimed, "The communications industry is taking a historic, first-of-its-kind step to beat poverty, injustice and inequality" as "the six biggest communications businesses in the world . . . agreed to put their differences aside in support of a joint unique and exciting initiative to advance the 2030 Agenda for Sustainable Development and the SDGs" (United Nations, 2016, para.2). More recently, in September 2018, the UN launched the SDG "Media Compact," an initiative marking a new drive to advance awareness of the SDGs in the media industry. This latter initiative "seeks to inspire media and entertainment companies around the world to leverage their resources and creative talent to advance the Goals" (United Nations, 2018, para.1). "Together, we commit to playing our part to achieve the Sustainable Development Goals," said Olusola Momoh, chairwoman, Channels Media Group-Nigeria at the launch event. "We are an alliance of news and entertainment media and we are committing to work with the United Nations to foster public discourse and spur action on the Sustainable Development Goals" (para.2).

This chapter examines the contribution of the six marketing companies involved in the Common Ground initiative and that of four leading media companies. Some of these companies operate in both the marketing and media industries, and they come from different parts of the world and are of varying size and reach. Dentsu was originally founded in 1901 and is based in Japan, employing some 50,000 people, with over 700 subsidiary companies, including the Dentsu Aegis Network, the multinational media and digital marketing company headquartered in London. WPP claims to be the world leader in communications services, employs over 194,000 people, and operates out of some 3,000 offices in 122 countries. WPP's activities include public relations and public affairs, advertising, branding and identity, health-care communications, media investment management and relationship marketing. The *Publicis Groupe* is a French based multinational advertising and public relations company, with some 78,000 employees worldwide. Havas is also a French-based multinational advertising and marketing company, and it has over 19,000 employees and operates in over 100 countries. The Omnicom Group, based in New York and founded in 1968, is a global marketing and corporate communications holding company, and its portfolio includes global advertising agency networks, media services provision and brand management. IPG is an advertising company that consists of three major networks – namely, McCann Worldgroup, Lowe & Partners and FCB – and employs some 50,000 people. Walt Disney Company, often known as simply Disney, is an American diversified multinational mass media and entertainment organisation, with headquarters in Burbank, California. Virgin Media is a British company, providing telephone, television and Internet services in the United Kingdom, with headquarters in Hook, Hampshire. Sky Limited is a British media and telecommunications conglomerate, with headquarters in London. It has operations in the United Kingdom, Ireland, Germany, Austria, Switzerland, Italy and Spain. The company had over 30,000 employees in 2018 with revenues of almost £13 billion in 2017. ITV plc is a British media company based in London, England. It holds 13 of the 15 regional television licences that make up the ITV network. ITV plc had revenues of over £3 billion in 2018 and is listed on the London Stock Exchange, being a member of the FTSE 100 Index.

Overview of marketing and media companies and the SDGs

The companies reviewed here vary in their approach to the SDGs (Table 5.1). Several companies targeted just one of the SDGs. Omnicom, for example, identified support of SDG4 as its principal contribution to the SDGs. The company noted (Omnicom, 2018) that it "has been simultaneously supporting global and local education programs while managing several projects with its newest partners to further deliver on the important promise of SDG4: inclusive and quality education for all" (para.2). John Wren, president and CEO of Omnicom Group, observed that "given our long history supporting educational initiatives, we are honored to be able to extend our support to two outstanding non-profits, Theirworld and Girl Effect, who share a similar mission – education for all" (para.3). WPP has emphasised its commitment to SDG5 – namely, to achieve gender equality and to empower all women and girls. In 2018, the company announced a partnership with UN Women, a global champion for gender equality, to "set a new agenda on equality through creativity" (WPP, 2018, para.4). In celebrating this announcement, Phumzile Mlambo-Ngcuka, executive director, UN Women, claimed,

> Changing how women and girls are seen and valued is fundamental to creating a more equal world. The marketing and advertising industry, which is so influential in shaping culture, is a key partner for us in this effort. With WPP, we are building both awareness and game-changing action to address gender inequality. Our work with WPP comes at the perfect time, as unprecedented numbers of women are mobilising worldwide on equality issues, ranging from ending violence and sexual harassment to calling for equal pay. This collaboration brings us both powerful imagination and industry muscle.
>
> *(WPP, 2018, para.3)*

Michael Roth, chairman and CEO of IPG, reported that the company had adopted SDG6 as one that the company would, in particular, pursue and support. More expansively, he argued, "Investments in sustainability align with the values of our clients and consumers," and he claimed, "The UN SDGs, and specifically water and sanitation, sit at the center of so many global issues" (IPG, 2017, para.3). In addition, the CEO asserted,

> Due to population growth and development, there's not enough sufficient clean, safe water to meet what's needed on a global basis. This scarcity impacts families, and ultimately economic and political stability, which affects businesses like ours as well as the quality of life for millions of people around the world. Advertising is a powerful tool, and we are proud to do our part in raising awareness around this issue, and in making a difference in the communities where we live and work.
>
> *(para.3)*

Havas (2018) argued, "Climate change is an urgent challenge to humanity that needs our immediate attention and action" and that "this is critical to the continuation of our society and business" (para.1) and primarily committed itself to SDG13. At the same time, Havas claimed, "We don't want people to feel overwhelmed when thinking about climate change. We want our collaborators and communities to feel empowered and take action by providing our resources to continually create innovative approaches to this issue" (para.3).

By way of contrast, Publicis (2018) chose to focus its energies on ten of the SDGs. The company notes,

> *Publicis Groupe* has responded to the appeal of the United Nations for more sustainable and inclusive enterprise models, which contribute to the success of the Sustainable Development Goals (SDGs). We have chosen to focus our efforts and increase our impact on the 10 goals.
>
> *(para.1)*

TABLE 5.1 SDGs addressed by marketing and media companies

SDG/ media company	Dentsu	Havas	Disney	Omnicom	Publicis	SKY	ITV	IPG	Virgin Media	WPP
1	x									
2	x				x					
3	x		x		x	x			x	
4				x	x	x				
5	x				x	x	x		x	x
6			x		x			x		
7						x			x	
8			x		x		x		x	
9						x				
10	x				x		x		x	
11										
12	x		x		x	x	x		x	
13		x			x	x	x		x	
14						x				
15						x				
16					x	x			x	
17	x				x	x	x			

The company adds, "Our approach is pragmatic and directly linked to social, societal and environmental responsibilities that are already part of our Group strategy" (para.2). The company highlighted SDGs 2, 3, 4, 5, 6, 10, 12, 13, 16 and 17 for their support. In addressing SDG13, for example, Publicis (2018) argues that it would "lend its support to behavioral changes in favor of responsible consumption; raising awareness of sustainability challenges in order to evolve everyone's actions and assure a positive impact, is an important objective in relation to our activities" (para.4). Further, the company suggests, "Improving best practices and evolving buying and sourcing are part of a vision in favor of a more just, integrated and efficient economic and social ecosystem" (para.4). In addressing SDG 5, Publicis suggests "equality between men and women" is fundamental to the company and that "a voluntary approach towards internal diversity of our teams is permanent, it involves being vigilant against all forms of discrimination" (para.4).

Dentsu (2018a) reports that it was focussed "on medium to long term megatrends," and engaged "in a variety of initiatives aimed at resolving global issues facing humanity" and that "we will contribute to the achievement of SDGs through the core business in the fields of marketing and communications" (para.3). More specifically, Dentsu identified three megatrends – namely, the redistribution of wealth, demographic change and digitisation and then mapped a number of the SDGs on to these trends. In addressing the first of these megatrends, Dentsu recognised its responsibilities in contributing to the development of countries throughout the world and in mapping this commitment on to SDGs 1 and 2 and suggested that the company was engaged in a variety of projects concerning poverty and income distribution. In a similar vein, Dentsu mapped its concern for the impact of demographic change on to SDGs 5, 10 and 12. Here the company claims it would "leverage its marketing and communication capabilities focused on advertising to raise consumer awareness and inspire action, significantly contributing to the creation of societies where everyone can live comfortably" (Dentsu, 2018a, para.5). The company also outlined a number of specific initiatives, discussed next, that can be seen as supporting SDGs 3, 10 and 17.

Virgin Media set out five long-term goals for the period 2015–2020 in their "Sustainability Performance Review" (Virgin Media, 2018). They called this their "5 in 5 plan" (Figure 5.1), and these goals are closely related to a number of the SDGs. The company's "Transforming Lives" initiative can be viewed in the context of SDGs 8, 10 and 16. The company notes that in 2018, 100,000 disabled people gained online access, including to disability employment content, and that the company's target for 2020 is that "1 million disabled people have the skills and confidence to get into and stay in work by the end of 2020." Their "more inclusive" objective can be seen as in support of SDG5 and aimed to "make progress towards 50:50 gender balance across the organisation (increase on 30%)" in 2018, and to "nurture an engaged workforce which represents the diversity of our customers and communities" in 2020. The "lower impact" objective is in support of SDGs 12 and 13 in particular, and attempted in 2018 to "grow our business without increasing our carbon footprint, maintain a zero waste to landfill logistics supply chain and increase office landfill diversion, (and) develop a plan to reduce plastic waste across our business" (p. 23).

Sky (2017) comments,

> Best practice organisations analyse how their business practices impact on society and the environment through a materiality process and then focus their sustainability programmes on those issues which matter most to the business and its stakeholders. By their nature, these material issues do not include all sustainability topics and therefore not all Sustainable Development Goals will be relevant.
>
> *(p. 1)*

The company identifies SDGs 3, 4, 5, 7, 8, 9 and 12–17 as those of which "map to Sky's material issues and reporting" (p. 3). For each of these goals, the company identifies which of the targets are of relevance to Sky and what the company will do to support them.

As regards Disney, Farquharson (2017) points out that "notable North American brands such as Apple, Walmart, Boeing and Disney have no references to the Sustainable Development Goals in their 2016 annual reports" (para.5). However,

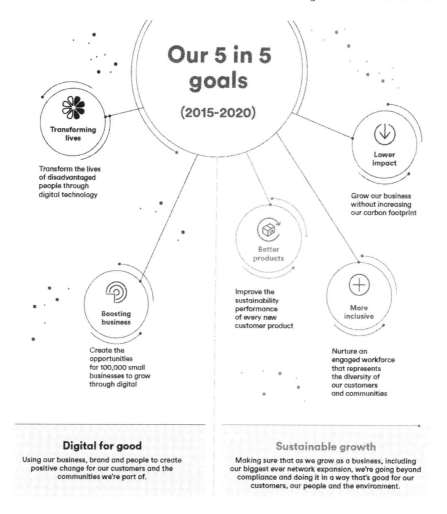

FIGURE 5.1   Virgin Media's "5 in 5" sustainability goals

Source: Virgin Media, 2019, p. 5.

in 2009, Disney had already announced a set of ambitious long-term goals around energy and carbon emissions, ecosystems, waste and water to reduce the company's environmental impact. The company notes,

> Business operations are reliant on natural resources and we recognize the importance of conserving and utilizing these resources responsibly. Healthy forests are a natural solution for sequestering carbon efficiently and cost-effectively, while providing many other valuable benefits. By improving the valuation of natural systems, Disney may also be able to make strategic investments in natural solutions that support efficient resource use.
>
> *(United Nations, 2017, para.2)*

By 2015, Disney had committed "to fund reforestation projects, fund a forest management project and to conduct a pilot study to quantify ecosystem benefits and services" (para.1) and has since identified particular targets relating to SDGs 3, 6, 8 and 12 that they will support and promote (US Council for International Business, 2018).

Somewhat similarly, ITV focusses more on their own sustainability initiatives rather than the SDGs *per se*. The company notes, "Our CR Strategy focuses on three priorities: People, Planet and Partnerships," and "these three pillars are underpinned by core responsible business practices" (ITV, 2017, p. 3). This strategy can be seen to align, for example, with SDGs 5, 8 and 10 (the people-related actions), SDG 12 and 13 (planet-related actions) and SDG 17 (partnership-related actions).

Actions and activities regarding specific SDGs

Under the banner "Transforming the Future," Dentsu (2017) reported on its contribution to the SDGs in 2016. In making this initial report, the company suggested that its approach to the SDGs was developed following extensive stakeholder consultation. This approach "uses the strength of our unique operating model to innovate the way brands are built in the health space" to address five "health priorities" (p. 6). These initiatives, which can be seen as in support of SDGs 3, 10 and 17, are to "end communicable diseases, reduce non-communicable mortality, reduce maternal and new-born mortality, promote mental health and well-being" and to "tackle ant-microbial resistance." Three intended outcomes were identified: "raising awareness, changing attitudes," and "delivering behavioural change," and in pursuing these outcomes, Dentsu looked to form partnerships with non-governmental organisations and local clients. More specifically, Dentsu (2017) illustrated its achievements with a number of cameo case studies. In the "Shared Heartbeats" (p. 8) campaign in Hungary, the company worked with its client T-Mobile to help mothers connect with their young children via an app on a mobile watch, which could relay the mother's heartbeat through a specially designed doll to help soothe the baby. Dentsu suggested that this mobile-enabled technology could have an important role to play in parts of the world where infant mortality rates are high. Dentsu also reported on "The Mosquito Killer Billboard" (p. 14) initiative in Brazil. This initiative, undertaken during the 2016 Olympic and Paralympic Games, involved using mobile billboards to attract and kill mosquitos in an attempt to curb the spread of the Zika virus, which had affected some 1.5 million Brazilians in the previous year. The billboard emits carbon dioxide and a lactic acid solution to mimic human breathing and sweat, and mosquitos that are attracted to the billboard become trapped inside and eventually die. The "Transforming the Future" report also included details of campaigns to tackle HIV in the Philippines, cardiovascular disease in New Zealand and cancer in Australia.

In 2017, as noted earlier, Omnicom (2017a) announced its partnership with two leading non-governmental organisations to promote SDG4 – "Theirworld" and "Girl Effect" (para.1), both of which are committed to the mission of education for all.

Theirworld employs pilot research projects and campaigning to help to bring better health and education to children, while Girl Effect uses mass media technology to help create a world where girls, no matter where they live, have the information and inspiration to seek out work and to demand the services they require to lead more fulfilled lives. A short video is used, and the underlying message is "it's clear that access to quality education can reduce poverty, save lives and protect the planet." In the video (Omnicom, 2017b), Sarah Brown, president of Theirworld, argued that Omnicom was "dedicated to education, dedicated to reaching that UN goal and that the company brought creativity, the strategic skills and the global reach" to the partnership.

In support of SDG5, WPP announced that their gender equality project is to be piloted across six countries – namely, the United States, the United Kingdom, India, Turkey, Thailand and Mexico. Here a number of WPP agencies have committed themselves to providing unpaid strategic, creative and media support during two key moments in UN women's calendar – namely, "International Women's Day in March and 16 Days of Activism Against Gender Based Violence in November" (WPP, 2018, para.6). In supporting these initiatives, Lindsay Pattison, chief transformation officer at WPP claimed,

> Together with UN Women, our mission is to empower women and raise awareness of important gender equality issues. As the world leader in communications services, WPP has the power and creative capability to help make the lives of women better across the world.
>
> *(para. 7)*

In the context of SDG6, IPG (2017) released a two-minute video, which features a case study of the importance of access to water and sanitation and outlines some of the work IPG is doing with non-governmental organisations and clients. The video claims that peace and healthy and accessible communities begin with water and emphasises "we are in the middle of a global water crisis" as reflected in the reality that "one in nine people don't have access to safe clean drinking water" and that "20% of the deaths under the age of five are due to water related disease." In looking to ameliorate this problem, the video suggests that need to construct "solutions around infrastructure, sanitation and hygiene" and by "protecting and restoring ecosystems." Towards the end of the video, IPG claimed "when it comes to solving the world's water issues, IPG aims to be part of the solution."

Virgin Media have taken a number of specific actions in support of their "5 in 5" plan discussed earlier. In support of the company's Transforming Lives initiative (and SDG10), they note that they are

> particularly proud of our work with (the disability charity) Scope. In 2017, we strengthened our partnership to drive even greater change for disabled people in the UK, focusing on closing the disability employment gap and supporting 1 million disabled people to get into and stay in work by the end

of 2020. We brought our partnership to life for our customers through the donation of our Southampton FC shirt sponsorship to Scope, generating over 180 pieces of news coverage and improving Scope's brand awareness by 6%. And internally, we kicked off our own Disability Action Plan to ensure that when it comes to building a more inclusive workplace, we step up and lead as an employer.

(*Virgin Media, 2018, p. 2*)

The company also suggest (M. Cobb, personal communication, July 31, 2019) that new initiatives show support for SDGs 3, 5 and 7. These include commitment to RE100 (the 100% renewable energy plan), incorporating electrical vehicle charging into their network infrastructure and the company's "Thrive" programme – a new collection of tools and resources to help staff be their best self at work and at home.

Havas (2018), in support of SDG13, reported on three specific initiatives: "LA Cool," "*L'Appel Des Solidarities*" and "Climathon." In the first of these initiatives, six Havas agencies in Los Angeles partnered with Climate Resolve, a nongovernmental organisation, to help shift the perception of climate change from a mere consumption tax to a real cultural conversation. The concept essentially looks to engage millennials in climate conversations through the outlets that resonate with them – namely, the city's art, food, music and pop culture. The Climathon initiative looks to stimulate climatic entrepreneurship, while *L'Appel Des Solidarities* was designed to promote environmental solidarity. Virgin Media (2018) have launched new driver monitoring software that "will deliver a reduction of 1 million litres of fuel a year" (p. 5). They also note that they have reduced paper use for the fourth year running and are "8% below our 2014 carbon baseline, a reduction of 18,000 tonnes of CO_2e." In Ireland, the company rolled out new cooling systems in their data centres and "introduced more efficient power by switching equipment that reduces power loads by 15%" (p. 5).

Discussion

A number of issues emerge from the previous review. First, there has been an apparent step change in the attitude and approach of marketing and media companies to sustainability and the SDGs. Hitherto, for example, the United Kingdom's Chartered Institute of Marketing (2006) concluded that "there is little evidence of a structured, strategic approach to marketing which acknowledges sustainability" (p. 17). Mont and Power (2010) recognised that marketing encourages high levels of material consumption, but they also argued that such strategies could just as easily be used to promote environmentally sound products and more sustainable lifestyles. This change to a more proactive support of sustainability and the SDGs is evidenced in the recent activities of companies outlined earlier.

Second, there is something of an *esprit de corps*, a collective effort, in both the marketing and media industry's approach to addressing the SDGs positively. This is evidenced in the "Common Ground" and "Media Compact" initiatives. In addition, Dentsu (2018b) has developed a corporate "Communications Guide" for the SDGs, which has been designed to assist "the managers of companies, the employees in charge of advertising, publicity and promotions, and everyone at advertising companies" (p. 1). This looks to provide guidance for the corporate world and outlines the pitfalls of what is described as "SDG Wash" (p. 12) – i.e. a superficial and non-effective approach to the SDGs. In addressing "advertising communication using the SDGs to improve corporate value," the focus is on "gaining a good reputation from society and customers" (p. 10) and the Guide offers a range of advice. Internally, within companies, Dentsu suggested that "SDGs become the common language of in house integration" and that such an approach will "accelerate promotion of the SDGs by gaining good corporate brand evaluation from society and customers and the SDGs become a common language that indicates the future of the company" (p. 10). In focusing on a range of external stakeholders, including other companies, not-for-profit organisations and local governments, the guide suggested that the SDGs could provide an important vehicle for "diverse collaboration and potential." At the same time, Dentsu also suggested that "when launching and notifying businesses aimed at the solution of social issues, if the business is evaluated and understood from a high viewpoint, then this contributes to promotion of the business" (p. 10).

Third, and notwithstanding the previous point, there is an evident contrast between those companies that are addressing the SDGs "head-on" and those that are sticking with their existing sustainability policies and addressing the SDGs implicitly and less directly; those that do address the SDGs directly vary considerably in the extent to which they actively support them. Havas, Omnicom, IPG and WPP target just one (and in each case a different one) of the SDGs, whilst Dentsu and Publicis reported looking to address five and ten of the SDGs, respectively. Sky identified 12 of the SDGs for their active support, and Disney has identified specific targets linked to 4 SDGs that they are addressing. On the other hand, Virgin Media and ITV have developed their own sustainability objectives based on concepts similar in nature to those underpinning the SDGs – "people," "planet," "partnership," transforming lives," "more inclusive" and "lower impact" – feature in these two companies' sustainability objectives. This varied approach perhaps reflects the nature of marketing and media businesses, where companies are often involved in a range of distinct but overlapping business activities, with contrasting strategies and multiple end products.

Conclusion

The evidence from the companies studied in this chapter suggests that the marketing and media industries recognise the need to accommodate – if not yet fully embrace – sustainability and the SDGs. Henderson (CSRwire, 2013) notes that although the "global advertising industry has encountered increasing criticism for promoting unsustainable consumerism," there was evidence that "a new ethic is afoot in the industry" which was spearheading "advertising's transition to sustainability" and was being led by "a new wave of creative agencies and practitioners" (para.1).

It is equally clear that the SDGs can be productively incorporated into business strategy and operations. Michael Roth, chairman and CEO of IPG, notes, "Sustainability is a significant opportunity for our company as we efficiently manage resources while driving employee innovation and profitability" (IPG, n.d., para.3), and Dentsu (2018b) concludes that the "opportunities for the SDGs to be used in public relations are increasing" (p. 17). More generally, the companies studied emphasise the importance of the creativity, strategic skills and global reach they bring to the SDGs, and the continuing need to integrate the SDGs into corporate management strategies.

References

Chartered Institute of Marketing. (2006). *Sustainable consumption and production: The role of marketers – final report.* Retrieved May 4, 2019, from www.mpgintl.com/papers/CIM%20 Final%20Report_-_Jun%202006.pdf

CSRwire. (2013). *Advertising's transition to sustainability.* Retrieved July 5, 2016, from www. csrwire.com/blog/posts/680-advertisings-transition-to-sustainability

Dentsu. (2017). *Transforming the future.* Retrieved May 1, 2019, from www.dentsu.com/csr/ pdf/transforming_the_future.pdf

Dentsu. (2018a). *Contributing to sustainable development goals.* Retrieved May 1, 2019, from www.dentsu.com/csr/reports/2017/esg/governance/sdgs.html

Dentsu. (2018b). *SDGs communication guide.* Retrieved October 24, 2018, from www.dentsu. com/csr/team_sdgs/pdf/sdgs_communication_guide.pdf

Farquharson, M. (2017). *Why Supporting the Sustainable Development Goals Is Good for Business.* World News. June 7. Seattle.

Havas. (2018). *Common ground.* Retrieved April 30, 2019, from www.globalcommonground. com/contributors/havas

IPG. (2017). *IPG releases video in support of SDG#6.* Retrieved June 16, 2019, from www. interpublic.com/about/stronger/strongerpost?id=10024

IPG. (n.d.). *General standard disclosures: Strategy & analysis.* Retrieved June 16, 2019, from www. interpublic.com/about/stronger/gri/report/indicator?report_id=1&subsection_id= 1&indicator_id=1

ITV. (2017). *ITV responsibility: Corporate responsibility summary report 2017.* Retrieved June 16, 2019, from http://itvresponsibility.com/resources/itv-corporate-responsibility-report-2017/

Mont, O., & Power, K. (2010). The role of formal and informal forces in shaping consumption and implications for a sustainable society. Part 1. *Sustainability, 2*(5), 2232–2252.

Omnicom. (2017a). *Omnicom expands commitment to UN sustainable development goals with the launch of two new multi-year global partnerships.* Retrieved April 30, 2019, from http://investor. omnicomgroup.com/investor-relations/news-events-and-filings/investor-news/news-details/2017/Omnicom-Expands-Commitment-To-The-UN-Sustainable-Develop ment-Goals-SDGs-With-The-Launch-Of-Two-New-Multi-Year-Global-Partner ships/default.aspx

Omnicom. (2017b). *Common ground partnerships: Girl effect and their world.* Retrieved May 2, 2019, from www.youtube.com/watch?v=vAbfxNFSz5U&feature=youtu.be

Omnicom. (2018). *SDG 4: Taking the lead on education*. Retrieved May 2, 2019, from http://csr.omnicomgroup.com/sdg4/

Publicis. (2018). *Sustainable development goals*. Retrieved April 30, 2019, from http://publicis groupe-csr-smart-data.com/en/sdgs/

Sky. (2017). *Sustainable development goals (SDGs): How the work of Sky PLC and the bigger picture strategy maps to the SDGs*. Retrieved April 2, 2019, from Sustainable%20Development%20 Goals_GG261017.pdf

United Nations. (2016). *Secretary-general announces common ground initiative, with advertising's 'Big Six' supporting sustainable development goals*. Retrieved June 17, 2019, from www.un.org/press/en/2016/envdev1683.doc.htm

United Nations. (2017). *Investing in Natural Solutions*. Sustainable Development Goals Partnerships Platform. Retrieved October 8, 2019, from https://sustainabledevelopment.un.org/partnership/?p=713

United Nations. (2018). *About the SDG media compact*. Retrieved May 1, 2019, from www.un.org/sustainabledevelopment/goal-of-the-month/sdg-media-compact-about/

United States Council for International Business. (2018). *The Walt Disney company. Business for 2030: Forging a path for business in the UN2030 business agenda*. Retrieved May 1, 2019, from www.businessfor2030.org/the-walt-disney-company

Virgin Media. (2018). *Half time team talk: 2017 sustainability performance*. Retrieved April 27, 2019, from https://assets.virginmedia.com/resources/pdf/VM_HowWeDid2017.pdf

Virgin Media. (2019). *2018 sustainability performance*. Retrieved August 4, 2019, from https://assets.virginmedia.com/resources/pdf/how-we-did-2018.pdf

WPP. (2018). *WPP announces industry – leading partnership with UN women to help achieve gender equality through power of creativity*. Retrieved April 30, 2019, from www.wpp.com/news/2018/09/wpp-announces-industry-leading-partnership-with-un-women

6

THE PHARMACEUTICAL INDUSTRY

Introduction

The global pharmaceuticals market was worth $934.8 billion in 2017 and will reach $1,170 billion in 2021, growing at 5.8% per annum (The Business Research Company, 2018a). The leading pharmaceutical companies come from the United States and Europe. Based on prescription sales, Pfizer is the world's largest pharmaceutical company, whilst other top global players from the United States include Johnson & Johnson, Merck & Co. and AbbVie. Novartis and Roche from Switzerland, GlaxoSmithKline (GSK) and AstraZeneca from the United Kingdom and French Sanofi are the leading European pharmaceutical companies. However, as in many other industries, the Chinese pharmaceutical sector has shown the highest growth rates over previous years.

Richard Saynor, senior vice president at GSK, has urged the big pharmaceutical companies to act decisively to improve global health and well-being to achieve the UN SDGs. He suggests, "On the part of pharmaceutical companies, we have a responsibility to help people gain access to high-quality healthcare and the medicines that they need, no matter where they live in the world or how much they can afford" (Pharma Boardroom, 2018, para.2).

This chapter examines the approach and contribution of ten globally operating pharmaceutical companies to the progression of the SDGs. Johnson & Johnson was founded in 1886 and is headquartered in New Jersey, USA. It has annual revenues of US$81 billion and is generally regarded as the largest pharmaceutical company in the world. The corporation includes some 250 subsidiary companies with operations in 60 countries and products sold in over 175 countries. Merck Sharp Dohme (MSD) was founded in 1891 and has its headquarters in New Jersey as well. The company employs 69,000 and has annual turnover in excess of US$40 billion. Pfizer was founded in 1849, with its headquarters based in New York City. It has annual revenues of US$52 billion and employs 96,500 staff. Eli Lilly has its headquarters in Indianapolis, Indiana. The company was founded in 1876 and now employs over

40,000 staff with annual revenues of over US$22 billion. Swiss company Roche was founded in 1896 and employees over 94,000 staff, with annual revenues of over 56,000 billion Swiss francs. Sanofi is a French multinational pharmaceutical company headquartered in Paris, with 110,000 staff and revenues of more than 34 billion euro. GSK is a British multinational pharmaceutical company headquartered in Brentford, London, and was established in 2000 by a merger of Glaxo Wellcome and SmithKline Beecham. The company has revenues of over £30 billion and more than 98,000 employees. AstraZeneca is a British-Swedish multinational pharmaceutical and biopharmaceutical company. It now has its headquarters in Cambridge, United Kingdom, and annual revenues of more than US$22 billion, employing 61,000 staff. Mylan is a global generic and specialty pharmaceuticals company registered in the Netherlands, with offices in Hatfield, Hertfordshire, United Kingdom and a "Global Center" in Pennsylvania, USA. It is the second-largest generic and specialty pharmaceuticals company in the world. Hikma originated in the Middle East but is now headquartered in London. The company specialises in generics and has annual revenues of more than US$2 billion.

Overview of the pharmaceutical industry and the SDGs

Most pharmaceutical companies are quite clear in their statements about which SDGs they are supporting in their business activities. GSK, for example, "recognises that collaboration is essential when it comes to tackling global health challenges which is why Goal 17 – Partnering – underpins a great deal of our work" (GSK, 2016a, para.2). Equally, however, the company notes

> Goal 3 has a specific focus on health and this is where the majority of GSK's work makes an important contribution. The goal is underpinned by targets that cover a wide range of health issues from maternal and child health to environmental health.
>
> *(para. 3)*

The company also adds that "although each of the 17 global goals is focused on a different issue, we believe that health underpins almost every development theme, each of which enables, or is enabled by, advances in population health" (para.3). Roche (2019a) supports a range of the SDGs but says that "as a global healthcare company, we are committed to supporting the SDGs in line with our business strategy; in particular SDG3, which aims at ensuring healthy lives and promoting wellbeing for all" (para.1). The company identifies SDGs 3–9, 12, 13, 16 and 17 as those in which they can make a particular impact. The focus on SDG3 is reiterated by Pfizer (2017), which states,

> Pfizer supports the SDGs and works to align its scientific focus and corporate objectives to improve global public health impact and sustainable development. Achieving good health and well-being is integral to all 17 of the goals,

and is specifically addressed in Goal 3, which states that every person deserves access to quality health care.

(p. 46)

Similar to Roche, Pfizer states that the company "is committed to helping achieve all 17 SDGs," but that "we combine our resources with the expertise of our partners to directly support progress toward several SDGs: 3, 5, 6, 9, 11, 12 and 17" (paras. 5/6).

MSD has a similar commitment. The company notes (MSD, 2018),

> As a global health care company that is committed to improving health and well-being around the world, SDG3 (Good Health and Well-Being) is at the core of our business and is aligned with our mission to save and improve lives. In addition, while we realize that all of the SDGs are essential to fostering sustainable development, we have prioritized eight global goals as those where we are positioned to have the biggest impact.
>
> *(paras. 5/6)*

In addition to SDG3, they identify SDGs 5–8, 12, 13 and 17 as "our eight priority SDGs" (para.7). However, they go a step further than some other pharmaceutical companies in that they identify from the 169 UN targets "11 targets for our priority SDGs that most closely align with our business" (para.8), and further, "we have identified existing metrics that enable us to quantitatively demonstrate our progress in support of the global goals" (para.7).

Johnson & Johnson (2019) claims that the company "was among the first private sector companies to announce a commitment toward achieving the 2030 Sustainable Development Goals (SDGs)" and that they "commit to galvanizing partners, mobilizing employees, and engaging communities to profoundly improve the course of human health through 2030" (para.1). The company is focusing on three main SDGs:

> We are dedicating our expertise, ideas and ingenuity to catalyze efforts toward achieving SDG3, Good Health and Well-being, which is at the heart of the Sustainable Development Goals and the core of our business. Our efforts will demonstrate the importance of Goal 5, Gender Equality, and will be founded in the principles of Goal 17, Partnerships for the Goals.
>
> *(para. 5)*

The company then identifies "five areas in which the Company is uniquely positioned to create sustainable and scalable impact" (para.6), with these being "health workforce," "women and children's health," "essential surgery," "global disease challenges" and "environmental health." Whilst there are aspirations and targets in all five areas, this represents a somewhat different approach to achieving the SDGs. This approach is similar to that adopted by Eli Lilly, which in its 2017 *Report on Progress* (Eli Lilly, 2017) notes that "throughout this report, we indicate where

TABLE 6.1 SDGs addressed by pharmaceutical companies

SDG/ pharma company	GSK	Astra Zeneca	Sanofi	Eli Lilly	Johnson & Johnson	MSD	Roche	Pfizer	Hikma	Mylan
1	x		x							
2	x		x	x						
3	x	x	x	x	x	x	x	x	x	x
4	x	x	x				x		x	x
5	x	x	x	x	x	x	x	x	x	x
6		x	x	x		x	x	x		x
7		x	x	x		x	x			
8	x	x				x	x		x	x
9	x	x	x				x	x	x	
10	x		x							
11								x		
12	x	x	x	x		x	x	x		x
13	x	x	x	x		x	x			x
14				x						
15	x	x								
16		x	x	x			x			x
17	x	x	x	x	x	x	x	x		x

our work aligns to the Sustainable Development Goals announced by the United Nations in September 2015. These intersections are noted by icons adjacent to relevant text" (p. 7). In this manner, they identify ten of the SDGs with which their business activities are aligned (Table 6.1).

Hikma (2018) focuses on fewer of the SDGs, noting that "while our activities contribute to a broad range of sustainable development themes, we have prioritized five SDGs that align most closely with our business and social engagement strategy" (p. 3), with these being SDGs 3, 4, 5, 8 and 9 (Figure 6.1). AstraZeneca (2016), on the other hand, adopts a broader perspective, saying that "as a healthcare company, we have an important role in contributing to the delivery of the UN Sustainable Development Goals (SDGs)" (p. 8). They identify SDGs 3–9 and 12, 13, 15, 16 and 17. They also note that "as we move forward with our strategy we will look to deepen our alignment and commitment to the SDGs" (p. 8). Similarly, Mylan (2017) claim to support 9 of the 17 SDGs. Sanofi (2017) confirms that the company "supports the more ambitious health objectives of the new Sustainable Development Goals (SDGs) covering 2016–2030" and that

> as a healthcare company, we are committed to scaling up our engagement to achieve health-related goals, such as those concerning infectious and

GOAL 3: GOOD HEALTH & WELL-BEING

- The launch of Hikma Specialized Oncology Unit
- Collaborating with the Royal Health Awareness Society

GOAL 4: QUALITY EDUCATION

- Support for the Sweimeh School for Girls
- Hikma's Continuing Education Programme
- The Children of Hikma Programme

GOAL 5: GENDER EQUALITY

- The Dare to Dream Big and Female Entrepreneurs Programme
- Addressing Gender Disparity within Hikma

GOAL 8: DECENT WORK & ECONOMIC GROWTH

- Operating Ethically and Supporting Inclusive Employment
- Providing Employment Opportunities across our Footprint

GOAL 9: INDUSTRY, INNOVATION & INFRASTRUCTURE

- Hikma's Contributions to Infrastructure and Economic Development
- Driving Innovation in the Healthcare Sector – Hikma Ventures
- Embedding a Corporate Culture of Innovation – ILAB

FIGURE 6.1 Hikma's focus on five SDGs

Source: Hikma, 2018, p. 2.

non-communicable diseases and universal health coverage. We are ready to provide our support through the development of new medicines and vaccines, but also through innovative partnerships in a wide range of areas: R&D, training for healthcare professionals, integrated access schemes for patients and disease management programs, etc.

(p. 1)

The report then highlights how the company is supporting 13 of the 17 SDGs with clear initiatives and direct action (Table 6.1).

Actions and activities regarding specific SDGs

Sanofi (2017) "supports the more ambitious health objectives of the new Sustainable Development Goals (SDGs) covering 2016–2030," and

> [we] are committed to scaling up our engagement to achieve health-related goals, such as those concerning infectious and non-communicable diseases and universal health coverage. We are ready to provide our support through the development of new medicines and vaccines, but also through innovative partnerships in a wide range of areas: R&D, training for healthcare professionals, integrated access schemes for patients and disease management programs, etc. . . . Our involvement at the highest level of the company in the Access Accelerated Initiative (AAI) is a way to upgrade our contribution to the SDGs in the fields of non-communicable diseases (NCDs). Through the AAI, Sanofi and other pharmaceutical companies pledge to commit to helping achieve the United Nations Sustainable Development Goals, and in particular, to reduce premature deaths from NCDs by one-third by 2030. During the launch of the initiative in January 2017 at the Davos Summit, Sanofi committed to contributing in the fields of diabetes, mental health and child cancer.
>
> *(p. 1)*

The company illustrates its support for the SDGs by citing a range of initiatives, projects and programmes, and this is paralleled by most other pharmaceutical companies reviewed here.

For SDG1, for example, Pfizer's "RxPathways" program helps eligible patients in the United States, Puerto Rico and the Virgin Islands get access to Pfizer medicines by offering a range of support services. More than 40 brands are now offered for free through the programme, and over the last 5 years, the programme "has helped nearly 2.5 million patients to access more than 30 million Pfizer prescriptions." In addition, Pfizer has a number of other projects aimed at increasing access to medicines, including its "International Trachoma Initiative and Diflucan Partnership Program (which provides treatment for AIDS related fungal infections in developing countries)" (UN Global Compact & KPMG, 2016, p. 14). Similarly, through the ZINA health project in Madagascar, "Sanofi and the NGO Positive Planet are committed to developing innovative solutions to help provide access to healthcare for disadvantaged populations, particularly in Madagascar, through the creation of micro-insurance systems" (Sanofi, 2017, p. 2).

SDG3 is arguably the most supported by the pharmaceutical companies, and some see this as central to their business vision. All ten companies included in the study supported this SDG, as did Japanese multinational Takeda, the largest pharmaceutical company in Asia. The company notes,

> SDG3 aligns with Takeda's mission, which is to strive for Better Health and a Brighter Future for people worldwide through leading innovation

in medicine. Therefore we believe that all of Takeda's business activities will contribute to achieving the aforementioned goal.

(Takeda, 2018, p. 6)

Other pharmaceutical companies are very specific in detailing particular targets relating to the SDGs and how they are monitoring their own performance against these targets. Sanofi (2017) cites the Ghana Accessibility and Affordability Programme, which

> is a public private initiative (involving Ghana authorities, the Bill & Melinda Gates Foundation, other pharma companies and other partners), which aims to provide access to effective, safe and affordable medicines for the treatment of non-communicable diseases (NCDs). The initiative is targeting underserved Ghanaians of low and middle-income socio-economic status suffering from NCDs such as diabetes, hypertension and cancer.
>
> *(p. 4)*

MSD (2018) identities three main UN targets they are pursuing to progress SDG3. For target 3.1 (reduce the global maternal mortality ratio to less than 70 per 100,000 live births), for example, the company cites the "MSD for Mothers" project, a "10-year, $500 million global initiative to create a world where no woman dies giving life." The company states that in 2017, over 2.9 million women received "improved quality of care through MSD for Mothers," and that by "contributing our scientific and business expertise, as well as our financial resources, we are working to ensure that women have access to two of the most powerful means to end preventable maternal deaths: quality maternity care and modern contraception." The company also claims that meeting women's needs in these two areas will reduce maternal deaths by 73% from 2017 levels, noting

> over the past six years, MSD for Mothers has reached more than 6 million women in over 30 countries around the world, contributing to the global effort to save women's lives, strengthen health systems and meet the United Nations' Sustainable Development Goals.
>
> *(MSD, 2018, para. 9)*

For target 3.7, ensure universal access to sexual and reproductive health-care services, including for family planning, information and education and integration of reproductive health into national strategies and programmes – the company claims that

> in developing countries that have high rates of maternal mortality and low rates of contraceptive prevalence, we have created a sustainable business model to promote access to contraceptive health programs. These activities are focused primarily on sub-Saharan Africa and countries in Asia and Latin

America with high unmet need. Through this model, we work closely with core global partners and their regional and local affiliates.

(para. 10)

As regards target 3.B – support the research and development of vaccines and medicines for the communicable and non-communicable diseases that primarily affect developing countries and provide access to affordable essential medicines and vaccines – MSD cites a number of initiatives. The company is "working to find new ways to bring our medicines and vaccines to more people around the world than ever before, and to make them as accessible and affordable as possible for the patients who need them." In addition, they "strive to commercialize our products in a way that both develops our business and meets local needs in a responsible and efficient manner," and to this end, "we have differential pricing for 42 of our products, and 125 countries have implemented inter- or intra-country pricing for at least one of our products" (para.11).

Roche (2019b) similarly supports SDG3 via a number of projects and initiatives. To improve global access to health care, they cite the Access Accelerated initiative, which they are "proud to support and co-lead" (para.1). This is a "first-of-its-kind cross-industry collaboration between 24 healthcare and biopharmaceutical companies," which aims to "to improve the prevention, care and treatment of non-communicable diseases (NCDs) through our medical solutions." The company notes that it is "committed to helping achieve the United Nations Sustainable Development Goals and have targeted the reduction of premature deaths from NCDs" (paras. 2/3). Roche also supports Personalised Reimbursement Models (PRM), which "deliver benefits to multiple stakeholders by making full use of drug utilisation data." By using this data, PRM allows medicines to be priced in line with the benefit they deliver to patients in different indications and combinations. Roche believe that "PRM will accelerate patient access to innovation and reduce financial pressure on prescribing by enabling the benefit of a medicine to be better reflected in its price" (Roche, 2019c, para.2). The company has also introduced International Differential Pricing, which "aligns the prices public healthcare systems pay for our new medicines with the relative incomes of emerging markets and developing countries" (Roche, 2019c, para. 4).

AstraZeneca (2015), in the context of SDG3, cited "The Young Health Programme," which they define as "our global community investment initiative. It has a unique focus on young people and primary prevention of the most common non-communicable diseases (NCDs). We have engaged over 1.4 million young people through our Young Health Programme since 2010" (p. 14). They also reference their Healthy Heart Africa (HHA) programme as their "flagship access to medicines programme." They claim,

> through HHA we are helping to tackle a silent killer in parts of the world where access to healthcare is at its lowest. Over one million patients were screened for hypertension through Healthy Heart Africa in 2015. We

currently run affordability projects in countries across Latin America, the Middle East and Africa, Asia Pacific and the US.

(p. 14)

Eli Lilly (2017) similarly notes,

Lilly has an important role to play in improving global health. Our commitment includes working to extend the Lilly promise of caring and discovery to millions more people around the world, and partnering with leading experts and organizations to expand our reach. Our global health efforts focus on communities with limited resources and people who aren't typically reached by our traditional business operations.

(p. 13)

To accelerate the company's global health efforts, they cite the "Lilly 30 x 30" project, which they position as "a bold goal to increase access to quality health care in communities with limited resources for 30 million people on an annual basis by 2030." Initiatives will "include activities across three key areas: Pipeline, Programs, and Partnerships" (p. 14), for which considerable detail is provided.

Hikma (2018) cites a number of projects and initiatives for the SDGs that they specifically support. For SDG4, for example, they note, "Within our organization, we have instilled a culture of continuous learning and development for our employees. We also engage frequently with our local communities to improve educational access and quality to those that need it most" (p. 8). A specific project in support of this SDG is the Sweimeh School for Girls, which is located in the Balqa province, where less than half of women are enrolled in basic education (49%), and the female illiteracy rate is more than double that of males. In 2015, Hikma "decided to adopt the Sweimeh School for Girls, initiating a comprehensive effort to improve the school's infrastructure, elevate educational standards and improve the students' academic results." Some of Hikma's major contributions to improving the school include the following:

- Complete renovation of the school nursery
- Rebuilding the students' garden and play areas
- Renovating old and damaged infrastructure
- Providing access to clean, sanitized and safe water supply
- Providing access to refrigeration for the school cafeteria
- Renovating the surrounding infrastructure – such as paving the roads – so that students can safely access the school

(p. 10)

Concerning SDG6, GSK (2016b) notes,

We are committed to ensuring water is managed sustainably and equitably as a shared public resource. We carry out environmental testing on all our pharmaceuticals, including relevant consumer healthcare products, to generate data to support our submissions to Regulatory Agencies. We also set our own environmental emission limits to minimise GSK pharmaceuticals/compounds discharge from our manufacturing sites.

(p. 4)

For SDG7,

Sanofi has taken the initiative to achieve a 20% reduction in the combined scope 1 and scope 2 CO_2 emissions for industrial and R&D sites and sales force vehicles. To reach this goal, Sanofi has formed strategic partnerships with energy sector leaders, implemented renewable energy projects at our sites in India, and continued our vehicle policy, including the increase in eco-driving sessions.

(Sanofi, 2017, p. 11)

SDG12 aims to protect local ecosystems, and in this context, Sanofi (2017) has been "supporting take-back programs that collect unused and expired medicines from patients and inform consumers about their safe disposal. Sanofi has supported such programs in 15 countries, including Brazil, Colombia, Mexico, the Philippines, Saudi Arabia, Venezuela" (p. 12).

GSK also illustrates how some companies are aligning their own internal objectives and goals with the SDGs. For example, GSK (2016a) notes,

Climate change is one of the world's most pressing issues and a major threat to people's health and global economic development. By using resources more efficiently and collaborating with others to tackle these challenges, GSK has ambitious goals in place to reduce carbon, water and waste across its value chain from the sourcing of raw materials and the impacts of its own labs and factories, to the use and disposal of its products by patients and consumers. For example, more than 500 of our suppliers are now sharing practical ideas to improve energy efficiency impacts through our online supplier exchange platform. We are also making changes to chemical manufacturing processes. For example, one of our sites in Singapore now uses enzymes in the manufacturing of amoxicillin (one of the world's most widely prescribed antibiotics), a process which significantly cuts carbon emissions and reduces waste.

(p. 2)

They link these initiatives to SDGs 3, 12, 13, 15 and 17.

For SDG13, Eli Lilly (2017) has "set aggressive targets for improving energy efficiency and thereby reducing our GHG emissions." They "have an established global energy management program to ensure continuous improvement and advance progress towards our goals." They outline their "multi-faceted approach," which includes a range of initiatives. These include "designing for energy efficiency in new or updated processes and facilities," "evaluating and incorporating alternative energy sources, new technologies, and best practices for energy use and GHG emission reductions," and "participating in local, regional, and national forums to understand and integrate energy management best practice and to support responsible and cost-effective decision-making and policy development" (p. 30).

Sanofi (2017) cites the AAI initiative noted earlier in the context of SDG17. Under the Access Accelerated coalition, Sanofi will work together with 21 industry partners, the World Bank and the UICC. The objectives are to

- Share best practice gathered from our longstanding commitments and own projects
- Design and set up targeted pilot projects, with the objective of scaling up these projects over time
- Identify what is working and what is not, so that we can collectively improve on our efforts to overcome barriers to primary care delivery for NCD patients
- Nurture disease-specific partnerships, starting with the development of effective, sustainable cancer care delivery models in a number of pilot cities

(p. 16)

Sanofi's AAI commitment includes four flagship programmes developed with specific partners: FAST – Fight Against Stigma, in the field of mental health; My Child Matters, in the field of childhood cancer; KiDS and diabetes in Schools; and the Access and Affordability initiative – testing the impact of differential pricing for NCD treatments in Ghana and the Philippines.

Discussion

The review of available literature and company reports raises a number of issues worthy of discussion. First, all the pharmaceutical companies reviewed had a positive and inclusive approach to the SDGs, recognising the value of, and need for, partnerships, resonating with SDG17. For example, with reference to the SDGs as a whole, Hikma (2018) notes, "We are convinced that for us to succeed as a company, we need to enable and empower those around us to succeed as well" (p. 3). GSK (2016a) concludes,

> The UN Sustainable Development Goals set out a vision for ending poverty, hunger, inequality and protecting the Earth's natural resources by 2030. Realising this ambition will require private sector, governments and civil society to play their part and work together in new and innovative ways."

The company "recognises that collaboration is essential when it comes to tackling global health challenges which is why Goal 17 – Partnering – underpins a great deal of our work" (para.2).

Second, the companies reviewed also highlighted SDG3 as of particular importance for their active involvement – indeed, of the 17 SDGs, only SDG3 was identified by all ten companies as being one they would support and progress. However, recent research by Consolandi and Eccles (2018) suggests a somewhat different interpretation. Eccles (2018) notes, "Clearly there is substantial variation within the healthcare sector in terms of its importance to the SDGs," and he suggests that the biotech and pharma industries are particularly important for progressing SDGs 4, 6, 9, 11 and 14. He also notes that "the SDGs for which biotech and pharma are least relevant" are SDGs 1, 7, 8, 13 and 16. Having used a methodology "fundamentally based on a mapping of Sustainability Accounting Standards Board (SASB) material issues to the SDGs," Eccles concludes that "these findings show that an industry can contribute to the SDGs beyond the intuitively obvious, as illustrated by biotech and pharma for SDG3, which actually ranks behind their top five" (para.8). Eccles adds, "The virtue of this approach is that it broadens the view of companies regarding which SDGs they can contribute to" (paras. 8/9). Overall, all the SDGs were supported by one or more of the ten companies included in the review, but Eccles's analysis highlights the difficulties involved in assessing which SDGs are being actively pursued by the pharmaceutical companies.

Third, the nature of the industry's products means it can do a great deal to support many of the SDGs through projects and programmes that make these products more widely available than would otherwise be the case, particularly in the developing world. This is evident in the majority of examples cited by the pharmaceutical companies in support of SDGs 3 and 6, for example. At the same time, changing the way the pharmaceutical companies operate in terms of energy and water consumption, employment and procurement policies is also cited in support of SDGs 5, 8, 12 and 13.

Conclusion

The ten companies studied showed unanimous support for SDG3 and SDG5 and very strong support for SDG17 and SDG12. SDG3 speaks specifically of improving access to medicines for patients who need them most and ensuring healthy lives for all and SDG17 aims to foster partnerships at many different levels. As Saynor recently noted, "This is where a holistic approach and a collaborative global response, involving pharmaceutical companies, the scientific community, policymakers, healthcare funders and professionals, as well as other stakeholders, will make a difference" (Pharma Boardroom, 2018, para.8).

The pharmaceutical companies have a vital and central role to play in advancing implementation of the SDGs in the next decade, but this will require progression and coordination of other initiatives, notably at the local level in the developing world. The increase in antimicrobial resistance to drugs is a particularly challenging problem, which highlights the significance of the pharmaceutical industry in advancing SDG3. An estimated 700,000 people across the globe are dying each year of drug resistance to illnesses, such as bacterial infections, malaria, HIV/AIDS or tuberculosis. HMG and Wellcome Trust (2014, p. 5) estimate that without action, this figure could rise to ten million people every year by 2050.

References

AstraZeneca. (2015). *Sustainability at AstraZeneca*. Retrieved June 17, 2019, from www.astrazeneca.com/content/dam/az/our-company/Sustainability/Sustainability-at-AZ.pdf

AstraZeneca. (2016). *Securing our future: Our sustainability journey*. Retrieved February 25, 2019, from www.astrazeneca.com/content/dam/az/Sustainability/55229%20AZ_Our%20Sustainability%20Journey_AW6_V2.pdf

The Business Research Company. (2018a). *The growing pharmaceuticals market: Expert forecasts and analysis*. Retrieved March 25, 2019, from https://blog.marketresearch.com/the-growing-pharmaceuticals-market-expert-forecasts-and-analysis

The Business Research Company. (2018b). *Pharmaceutical drugs global market report 2018*. Retrieved June 17, 2019, from www.marketresearch.com/Business-Research-Company-v4006/Pharmaceutical-Drugs-Global-Musculoskeletal-Disorder-11518658/?progid=90731

Consolandi, C., & Eccles, R. (2018). *Supporting sustainable development goals is easier than you might think. Big idea: Leading sustainable organizations blog*. Retrieved February 15, 2019, from https://sloanreview.mit.edu/article/supporting-sustainable-development-goals-is-easier-than-you-might-think/

Eccles, R. (2018). *The importance of the healthcare sector to the sustainable development goals*. Retrieved February 7, 2019, from www.forbes.com/sites/bobeccles/2018/07/01/the-importance-of-the-healthcare-sector-to-the-sustainable-development-goals/#555cb49067a3

Eli Lilly. (2017). *Eli Lilly UNGC communication on progress*. Retrieved February 13, 2019, from www.unglobalcompact.org/system/attachments/cop_2018/463263/original/2017_Lilly_UNGC_COP.pdf?1525468719

GSK. (2016a). *Our commitment to the sustainable development goals*. Retrieved February 8, 2019, from https://ca.gsk.com/media/1301873/our-commitment-to-sustainable-development-update.pdf

GSK. (2016b). *GSK public policy positions*. Retrieved March 12, 2019, from www.gsk.com/media/2979/public-policy-on-the-sdgs.pdf

Hikma. (2018). *Hikma and the UN sustainable development goals: Contributing to global growth and prosperity*. Hikma Pharmaceuticals, Amman, Jordan. Retrieved June 17, 2019, from www.hikma.com/media/1596/sustainable-development-goals.pdf

HMG and Wellcome Trust. (2014). *Antimicrobial resistance: Tackling a crisis for the health and wealth of nations*. Retrieved June 17, 2019, from https://amr-review.org/sites/default/files/AMR%20Review%20Paper%20-%20Tackling%20a%20crisis%20for%20the%20health%20and%20wealth%20of%20nations_1.pdf

Johnson & Johnson. (2019). *Our SDG commitment*. Retrieved February 13, 2019, from www.jnj.com/sustainable-development-goals

MSD. (2018). *Corporate responsibility report 2017/8 – sustainable development goals (SDGs) – MSD responsibility*. Retrieved February 2, 2019, www.msdresponsibility.com/our-approach/reporting-frameworks/sustainable-development-goals/

Mylan. (2017). *2017 progress report on global social responsibility*. Retrieved February 8, 2019, from www.unglobalcompact.org/participation/report/cop/create-and-submit/active/417486

Pfizer. (2017). *Annual review – sustainable development goals*. Retrieved February 5, 2019, from www.pfizer.com/files/investors/financial_reports/annual_reports/2017/our-business-our-purpose/sustainable-development-goals/index.html

Pharma Boardroom. (2018). *How can pharma progress the sustainable development goals?* Retrieved June 2, 2019, from https://pharmaboardroom.com/articles/how-can-pharma-progress-the-sustainable-development-goals/

Roche. (2019a). *Sustainable development goals.* Retrieved February 9, 2019, from www.roche.com/sustainability/un-sdgs.htm

Roche. (2019b). *Access Accelerated Initiative.* Retrieved October 8, 2019, from https://www.roche.com/sustainability/access-to-healthcare/access-accelerated-initiative.htm

Roche. (2019c). *Innovative pricing solutions.* Retrieved October 8, 2019, from www.roche.com/sustainability/access-to-healthcare/innovative-pricing-solutions.htm

Sanofi. (2017). *Sanofi's commitment and contribution to the UN sustainable development goals.* Retrieved June 17, 2019, from www.sanofi.com/-/media/project/one-sanofi-web/websites/global/sanofi-com/home/common/docs/download-center/sanofis_commitment_and_contribution_to_the_un_sdgs_may_2017.pdf/

Takeda. (2018). *Sustainable value report 2018.* Retrieved February 8, 2019, from www.takeda.com/siteassets/system/csr/sustainable-value-report/report_2018_en.pdf

UN Global Compact and KPMG. (2016). *SDG industry matrix: Healthcare & life sciences.* Retrieved June 17, 2019, from https://home.kpmg/content/dam/kpmg/xx/pdf/2017/05/sdg-healthcare-life-science.pdf

7

THE RETAIL INDUSTRY

Introduction

Throughout much of the world, retailing provides the vital and continually evolving link between primary producers and manufacturers and consumers, makes a major economic contribution to national economies and is a major source of employment. The majority of the world's leading retailers have been pursuing sustainability strategies for some time, and there is growing awareness that retailers have a vital role to play in promoting the transition to a more sustainable future. It is evident that they are in a singularly powerful position to drive sustainable development in three ways: through their own actions, through partnerships with suppliers and through their daily interactions with consumers. Durieu (2003), for example, argues that large retailers "can greatly influence changes in production processes and consumption patterns and are well-positioned to exert pressure on producers in favour of more sustainable choices" (p. 7).

For some time, many leading retailers have publicly reported on their sustainability strategies and on their achievements in pursuing these strategies (Jones, Wynn, Comfort, & Hillier, 2007), but a growing number of large retailers are now increasingly looking to adopt the SDGs to provide a framework for addressing their contribution to the transition to a more sustainable future. Nevertheless, leading retailers seem likely to face some daunting challenges if they are to make a genuine contribution to the SDGs. In advertising its 2014 Bi-Annual Conference on Business and the Environment, for example, Globe, a not-for-profit organisation, posed the question, "Is the overarching need to reduce consumption simply at odds with the very foundation of retailing?" (Globe, 2014, p. 1). This chapter discusses how some of the world's leading retailers are publicly addressing and adopting the SDGs and reviews the challenges and contradictions inherent in some of their activities. The companies included in this review are Aldi, a German-owned, family-owned discount supermarket chain with over 10,000 stores in 20 countries and estimated annual revenues in excess of €50 billion; John Lewis & Partners, an employee-owned UK company which operates its department stores; the Waitrose & Partners supermarkets, its banking and financial services and other retail-related activities, with a turnover of more than £10 billion in 2018; Sainsbury's, founded in 1869 by John James Sainsbury with a shop in Drury Lane, now the third-largest chain of supermarkets in the United Kingdom, with a turnover of over £28 billion in 2018; Tesco, a British multinational groceries and general merchandise retailer, with shops in seven countries across Asia and Europe and now the third-largest retailer in the world with revenues of over £57 billion in 2018; Kroger, an American retailing company, the fifth-largest retailer in the world and the third-largest American-owned private employer in the United States with revenues of over US$115 billion in 2016); Walmart, an American multinational retail corporation that operates a chain of hypermarkets, discount department stores and grocery stores, operating in 27 countries, including Asda in the United Kingdom (Walmart is the world's largest company by revenue – with revenues of over US$500 billion in 2019); Target, the eighth-largest retailer in the United States, headquartered in Minneapolis, Minnesota, with revenues of over US$75 billion in 2019; Walgreens Boots Alliance, an American holding company headquartered in Illinois that owns Walgreens, Boots and a number of pharmaceutical manufacturing, wholesale and distribution companies, with revenues over US$131 billion in 2018; Metro AG, a German retail, wholesale and cash and carry group with revenues of €58 billion in 2016; and Rewe Group, a German retail cooperative group based in Cologne with revenues in excess of €57 billion in 2017.

Overview of leading retailers and the SDGs

In March 2018, 25 of the United Kingdom's leading retailers signed up to the British Retail Consortium's (2018) "Better Retail Better World" initiative, which aims for greater corporate alignment with the SDGs. The retailers included Aldi; Asda; the Co-operative; IKEA; John Lewis & Partners; Kingfisher; Marks & Spencer; Morrison's; NEXT; and Sainsbury's. As part of this initiative, individual retailers pledged to share knowledge and skills and publicly disclose progress on the SDGs. Ricard Pennycook, chair of the British Retail Consortium, claimed,

> This is part of a growing movement for change. It is time for the retail industry to show what it can do for the common good. We are taking collective action to build a better, more prosperous and sustainable world and demonstrate how we are making a positive contribution to society in terms of the supply chain, food packaging and waste.
>
> *(British Retail Consortium, 2018, para. 7)*

Tanya Steele, chief executive of the World Wide Fund for Nature, argued, "Retail businesses working with consumers are key to the success of the SDGs and key in the race to restore nature" (British Retail Consortium, 2018, para.11).

Some of the United Kingdom's leading retailers have initially targeted a number of the 17 SDGs (Table 7.1). Aldi (2018a), for example, highlights its commitment to nine of the SDGs – namely, SDGs 2, 3, 5, 6, 8, 12, 13, 14 and 17. John Lewis & Partners (2018a) reported, "We welcome the UN Sustainable Development Goals and are committed to contribute to a prosperous and resilient society in which our partners, customers and industry can thrive, within the means of our planet" (para.1), and identified SDGs 3, 6, 8, 10, 11, 12, 13, 15 and 16 as its priorities. The company matched these SDGs to its overall business strategy within a "corporate responsibility framework" that implied a "recognition of the need for a shift in ambition behind the areas we want to deliver progress on" (para.3). The SDGs that were identified for support aligned with the company's leadership in corporate responsibility through some key principles and activities: to "source and sell with integrity," "unlock partner potential" and "deliver more with less" (John Lewis & Partners, 2018b, p. 26; Figure 7.1). In their 2018 "Sustainability Update," Sainsbury's (J. Sainsbury, 2018) reported on how the company was contributing to all the SDGs, noting that "collaboration will accelerate progress towards achieving the SDGs" and "we're also continually looking at new opportunities for collaboration" (p. 21). The company orientates its support for the SDGs around several of its key company initiatives: "living healthier lives" (p. 10), "making a

TABLE 7.1 SDGs addressed by retail companies

SDG/ retailer	Aldi	John Lewis	Sainsbury's	Tesco	Walmart	Kroger	Target	Walgreens Boots Alliance	Metro	Rewe
1			x					x	x	
2	x		x	x	x	x		x	x	x
3	x	x	x	x		x		x	x	
4			x					x	x	
5	x		x		x		x	x	x	
6	x	x	x				x	x	x	
7			x	x	x			x	x	x
8	x	x	x	x	x	x	x	x	x	x
9			x					x	x	
10		x	x					x	x	
11		x	x				x	x	x	
12	x	x	x	x	x	x	x	x	x	x
13	x	x	x	x		x	x	x	x	
14	x		x	x	x	x		x	x	x
15		x	x	x		x		x	x	x
16		x	x					x	x	
17	x		x					x	x	

FIGURE 7.1   The John Lewis framework for the SDGs

Source: John Lewis, 2018b, p. 26.

positive difference to our community" (p. 11), "respect for our environment" (p. 12), "sourcing with integrity" (p. 14) and "great place to work" (p. 16). Tesco PLC (2018) also supports all 17 SDGs but identified SDGs 2, 3, 7, 8, 12, 13, 14 and 15 as their "priority goals" (p. 2).

Some, but certainly not all, of the leading US retailers have also emphasised their commitment to the SDGs, though there is no industry-wide coordination of these commitments. Under the banner "Business for 2030: Forging a Path for Business in the 2030 UN Development Agenda," Walmart (2018), the world's largest retailer, focussed on SDGs 2, 5, 7, 8, 12 and 14. Kroger (2018) reported that it "supports the direction and collaborative approach of the UN SDGs" and that "we recognise the importance of these collective global goals in achieving a future to which we all strive – where we can sustain, nourish and empower our growing world population while protecting our planet" (p. 24). The company notes that "we are particularly pleased to align our most ambitious work with Goal 2: Zero Hunger and Goal 12: Responsible Consumption and Production" (Kroger, 2018, p. 15), but in addition, the company stressed its belief that "because we are a grocery retailer with tremendous size and scale, we believe Kroger is uniquely positioned to contribute significantly to several key SDGs" (p. 24) – namely, SDGs 2, 3, 8, 12, 13, 14 and 15.

In a similar vein, Target (2018) claimed, "Our corporate responsibility strategy is guided by leveraging our business practices and decisions to help deliver on the UN SDGs." They "acknowledge the importance of all 17 SDGs" and claim that they "are actively working to initially drive deeper progress in six of the global goals where we feel we currently can make the greatest impact" (p. 40) – namely, SDGs

5, 6, 8, 11, 12 and 13. Walgreens Boots Alliance also reported that its CSR targets and activities were aligned with the UN SDGs and claimed, rather like Sainsbury in the United Kingdom, that "given our global presence and the scope of our business activities, we take the approach of addressing all of the SDGs" (Walgreen Boots Alliance, 2017, p. 17).

Public commitment to the SDGs amongst the leading retailers within the European Union has received less attention in the retailers' sustainability reporting process. While Metro (2018), for example, provided a brief outline of how it supports all 17 SDGs, Carrefour did not address the SDGs in its *2017 Annual Report*. In the introduction to the "Corporate Social Responsibility Section" of its "2017 Management Report," Auchan (2018) emphasised that "the 17 sustainable development goals set by the United Nations for the next decade remind us of the urgency of the global issues that we must address to ensure a prosperous and equitable future for future generations to come" (p. 3). Although the company did not specifically address the SDGs in the main body of the 80-page report, it, nevertheless, contains sections on topics that resonate with the SDGs – for example, "Encouraging Gender Equality" (p. 17), "Optimising Waste Management and Promoting the Circular Economy" (p. 24) and "Optimising and Reducing our Energy Consumption" (p. 28). Rewe Group (2018), referring to the SDGs, notes that it

> is determined to support the effort to reach these goals by carrying out its sustainability strategy. To do so, it has compared its sustainability goals and business processes with the 17 UN development goals and the related 169 SDG targets. Following this analysis, sustainability managers at Rewe Group prioritised the SDGs and targets

and "feedback provided by stakeholders was used in an overall ranking in which the following SDGs were given a high priority" (para.19). These were identified as SDGs 2, 8, 7, 12, 14 and 15.

A number of the major retailers elsewhere in the world have referred to the SDGs in their sustainability and CSR reports, but there is little evidence of a consistent or coordinated pattern of corporate commitment. Thus while Japan's leading retailer, Seven & I Holdings Co (2018), reported that it would respond positively to the UN SDGs, it did not provide any information on how its response would be carried forward.

Actions and activities regarding specific SDGs

In addressing SDG2, Walmart (2018) reported setting "a number of goals to contribute to ending hunger." The company "aspires to provide 4 billion meals to those who need them in the US from 2015 to 2020 via grants from the Walmart foundation and food donations from our Walmart stores," noting that to date "11 billion meals have been provided and $61 million has been contributed to organizations."

In addition, the company aimed "to open between 275–300 stores in 'food deserts' in the US by 2016: by the end of FY 2016, 375 stores serving food deserts were opened across the US" (para.2). At the same time, the company reported,

> As the world's largest food retailer, Walmart works with suppliers and many others along the food chain to strengthen sustainability – creating food system that is more affordable for people and planet, more accessible for all, healthier, safer and more transparent. Walmart and the Walmart foundation are committed to training 1 million farmers and farm workers by the end of 2016. To date, Walmart and the Walmart foundation have contributed to training 564,321 farm workers, 297,655 of whom were women.
>
> *(Walmart, 2018, para. 4)*

Somewhat similarly, in addressing SDG2, Tesco (2018) recorded,

> We work closely with food banks and charities wherever we operate to donate good food that would otherwise go to waste. Organisations we have supported have included homeless shelters, after-school clubs, food banks and domestic violence hostels. We also organise regular food collections during festive periods giving our customers the opportunity to join us in donating food to help feed people in need."

The company also stated, "48 million meals (were) donated Group-wide through our food surplus donation programmes in 2017/18" (p. 2). Sainsbury also reported that 73% of its stores had a food donation partner and noted the company's commitment "to achieve zero net afforestation by 2020, by responsibly sourcing key commodities such as soya, palm oil, paper and pulp and cattle" (J. Sainsbury, 2018, p. 19). In 2017, Kroger launched their "Zero Hunger/Zero Waste" social impact plan, which the company claims, "plays an important part in our support of global sustainable development." The objective is

> to end hunger in our communities and eliminate waste across our company by 2025. This directly aligns with SDG 2: Zero Hunger with our target to donate 3 billion meals by 2025–5 years ahead of the Global Goal. It also aligns with SDG12: Responsible Consumption and Production and our goal to achieve zero waste in our operations by 2020, zero food waste across our company by 2025, and to improve the sustainability of our product packaging.
>
> *(Kroger, 2018, p. 24)*

In the context of SDG3, Walgreens Boots Alliance (2017) notes that in 2017, the company "expanded its program to prevent opioid abuse and help fight the rise in overdose-related deaths working with government representatives around the country to change legislation and to implement solutions." The company claims, "Walgreens medication disposal program, launched in 2016, is the first on-going national effort of its kind by a retailer to combat the drug abuse crisis in the US" (p. 18). The company also reports on its activities to fight other diseases, notably cancer, aids, dementia and leukaemia, noting "we continue to support the important work of fund-raising, but we are also going beyond that to help with education, training and patient support" (p. 21). Somewhat by contrast, but again in support of SDG3, Aldi (2018b) notes, "In each of our countries of operation, we sustainably support effective social initiatives and offers" (para.2). In 2017, the company

> provided funding in the amount of approximately EUR 19.6 million in order to support charitable causes across all of our countries of operation. In addition, we donated various products with a total sales value of more than EUR 660,000. Practically all of our stores and regional distribution centres cooperate with organisations, which collect unsold food products and donate these to charitable causes. Also, more than 2,900 of our employees participated in corporate volunteering activities.
>
> *(para.3)*

For SDG5, Aldi (2018a) notes, "We do not tolerate any form of discrimination as these contradict the honest and respectful manner of interacting with each other that we perceive as a central element of our corporate culture." They add that "in all national business operations, men and women in identical positions receive equal pay. Moreover, all of our national business operations have established independent complaints mechanisms which employees may use if they feel discriminated against or in the event of other breaches of regulations" (para.10). Additionally, the company has its ALDI Factory Advancement Project PLUS by which "we support production facilities in Bangladesh towards improving their internal childcare offers to enable in particular women to pursue a career" (para.11).

Regarding SDG7, Tesco suggested "we have developed a roadmap and targets to source 65% of our electricity from renewable sources by 2020 and 100% by 2031" (Tesco, 2018, p. 2). For SDG8, Kroger (2018) notes, "Our health and safety initiatives in our facilities, the thousands of jobs we create each year and our commitment to protect human rights in our supply chain contribute to the objectives of SDG8: Decent Work and Economic Growth" (p. 24). In addressing SDG10, Sainsbury reported, "We support our farmers, growers and communities in our supply chain so that they can have thriving businesses for years to come" and that "in 2017 we launched our Fairly traded pilot scheme to help improve the livelihoods of large and small scale tea farmers in Eastern and southern Africa" (p. 20). Concerning SDG12, Tesco (2018) (Figure 7.2) notes,

> We have adopted UN SDG 12.3 to help halve food waste from farm to fork. We are proud members of Champions 12.3, a coalition of leaders chaired by our CEO Dave Lewis to accelerate progress on this target. In the UK and Central Europe we have sold nearly 25,000 tonnes of Perfectly Imperfect

SDG	Tesco Target	Tesco Action
12 RESPONSIBLE CONSUMPTION AND PRODUCTION	Help halve global food waste, farm to fork, by 2030.	We have adopted UN SDG 12.3 to help halve food waste from farm to fork. We are proud members of Champions 12.3, a coalition of leaders chaired by our CEO Dave Lewis to accelerate progress on this target. In the UK and Central Europe we have sold nearly 25,000 tonnes of Perfectly Imperfect fruit and vegetables that previously would not have met our specifications and have removed best before dates from over 180 UK fruit and vegetable lines to help stop perfectly edible items being thrown away.
	Making all packaging fully recyclable by 2025.	We want to create a closed loop system for packaging so everything can be re-used, recycled or re-purposed. We have committed to remove all hard to recycle materials from our Own Brand packaging by the end of 2019 and are working with our suppliers to find alternatives. For example, by replacing polystyrene, a hard-to-recycle material, with cardboard in our Own Brand pizzas we have saved 300 tonnes of plastic.
13 CLIMATE ACTION	Reduce absolute carbon emissions from our operations from 2015 levels: 35% by 2020, 60% by 2025 and 100% by 2060.	We have worked with external experts to set new, science-based targets which are aligned with a 1.6 degree trajectory and enable us to meet our zero-carbon ambition. As one of the largest van fleet operators in the UK we have signed up to the Clean Van Commitment (CVC). The commitment publicly demonstrates our support for the switch to low emission vehicles.
14 LIFE BELOW WATER	Sustainably source all our wild fish.	We are committed to supporting truly sustainable fisheries and the protection of marine environments. We are working with the Marine Stewardship Council (MSC) to increase our range of certified sustainable counter, pre-packed, canned and frozen fish. Beyond certification we have worked with the krill fishing industry and NGOs to develop an agreement that will protect vulnerable species and habitats in the Antarctic that rely on krill. Krill is an ingredient in salmon feed and some health supplements.
15 LIFE ON LAND	Achieve zero net deforestation in our supply chain by 2020.	We are working to reduce the impact of our beef, soy, palm, dairy, cotton and other key supply chains. We developed our Zero Deforestation Soy Transition Plan in consultation with leading NGOs to help achieve our aim to source all the soy-based animal feed in our UK supply chain from areas verified as having zero deforestation by 2025. We are supporting this with trials of more sustainable sources of animal feed such as algal oil and insect protein.

FIGURE 7.2 Tesco targets for priority SDGs 12–15

Source: Tesco, 2018, p. 3.

> fruit and vegetables that previously would not have met our specifications and have removed best before dates from over 180 UK fruit and vegetable lines to help stop perfectly edible items being thrown away.
>
> *(p. 3)*

In addressing SDG13, Aldi (2018a) claims, "Our climate protection goal is to reduce our greenhouse gas emissions – measured in carbon equivalents per square metre of sales floor – by at least 30% by 2020" (para.23). Similarly, Tesco (2018) set a target to "reduce absolute carbon emissions from our operations from 2015 levels: 35% by 2020, 60% by 2025 and 100% by 2050" (p. 3), and Kroger (2018) claims "Our investments in energy efficiency, reductions in refrigerant emissions and renewable energy installations, all advance the objectives of SDG13: Climate Action" (p. 24).

Target (2018) is actively pursuing six of the SDGs noted earlier through "four focus areas that help us improve the lives of families today and tomorrow: Empower Teams, Serve Guests, Foster Communities and Design Tomorrow" (p. 40), each with their own company goals. Although not explicitly stated several of these company goals align with the six SDGs. For example, in the context of SDGs

6, 12 and 13, under the "Design Tomorrow" focus area, the company will "drive energy and water efficiency in our own operations and in our supply chain." The company notes,

> Our energy efficiency programs are driven by significant investments in intelligent LED lighting systems in our stores, replacement of inefficient HVAC and refrigeration systems and smart building energy management systems to capture building efficiencies. Related to our operational water usage, Target is focused on water conservation initiatives including irrigation management and restroom fixture efficiencies.
>
> *(p. 45)*

In reporting on SDG14, Aldi (2018a) emphasised,

> We have increased the sustainability of our range of fish and seafood products. All national business operations have defined Corporate Buying Policies at national level, which are binding for both our suppliers and our Buying teams. We regularly review our range of fish and seafood products on the basis of external expertise – provided, among others, by representatives of Greenpeace and the Sustainable Fisheries Partnership (SFP) – taking into account aspects, such as species, catchment area, and catchment methods.
>
> *(para.25)*

Tesco (2018) highlights the fact that

> we are committed to supporting truly sustainable fisheries and the protection of marine environments. We are working with the Marine Stewardship Council (MSC) to increase our range of certified sustainable counter, pre-packed, canned and frozen fish. Beyond certification, we have worked with the krill fishing industry and NGOs to develop an agreement that will protect vulnerable species and habitats in the Antarctic that rely on krill. Krill is an ingredient in salmon feed and some health supplements.
>
> *(p. 3)*

For SDG17, Aldi (2018b) states,

> In each of our countries of operation, we sustainably support effective social initiatives and offers. For this purpose, we commit to long-term partnerships with selected charitable organisations, which, above all, provide services in the areas of education, health, nutrition, social affairs, and environmental protection.
>
> *(para.3)*

Discussion

A number of issues emerge from the review of the retailers' approach and positioning regarding the SDGs. First, there are several different approaches to the SDGs
taken by the companies studied here. Some of the retailers have addressed the SDGs
head-on (e.g. Walmart, Aldi and Tesco), some cluster them against their existing
CSR themes (e.g. John Lewis, Kroger) and one or two note support for the SDGs
but do not explicitly link them to their existing CSR policies (e.g. Auchan). This
reflects the fact that, prior to 2015, many retailers had already done a significant
amount of analysis of CSR priorities and "materiality," and have thus settled on
trying to retrofit the SDGs to their own existing CSR policies. Kroger, for example, maps out the relative priority of sustainability issues, and, clearly, some of the
"Tier 1" (Kroger, 2018, p. 25) topics align with some of the SDGs (e.g. energy and
emissions, food waste, responsible sourcing, diversity and equal opportunity). However, to re-orientate the company's CSR policy and reporting to be based upon the
SDGs may not be seen as a realistic proposition.

Second, the retail industry is ideally placed to address, above all, SDG12 – namely,
to ensure sustainable consumption and production (SCP). Retailers are the active
intermediaries between primary producers and manufacturers, on the one hand, and
consumers, on the other and as such they can be seen to be in a singularly powerful
position to drive sustainable consumption in three ways – through their own actions,
through partnerships with suppliers and through their daily interactions with consumers. For some time, there has been a growing awareness that retailers have a vital
role to play in promoting more sustainable patterns of consumption. The European
Commission (2019) argued, "Retailers in Europe are in an exceptional position to
promote more sustainable consumption not only via their daily contact with millions
of European customers but also through their own actions and partnerships with
suppliers" (para.6). Similarly, in its *Retail Sustainability Management Report*, the US
Retail Industry Leaders Association (2017) also identified sustainable consumption
as the most critical issue for retailers to address. However, there is little consensus in
defining sustainable consumption, and it is widely recognised to be a contested concept (Seyfang, 2004). Case studies of leading retailers in the United Kingdom (Jones,
Hillier, & Comfort, 2014) and the United States (Jones & Comfort, 2018) found that
leading retailers made few public corporate commitments to sustainable consumption. While all of the United Kingdom's top-ten retailers stressed their commitment
to sustainability on their corporate websites, any focus on sustainable consumption
was conspicuous primarily by its virtual absence from their sustainability and CSR
reports. Indeed, only two of the leading retailers made explicit reference to sustainable consumption. Similarly, in the United States, retailers' commitments to sustainable consumption revealed that the specific issue of sustainable consumption, *per se*,
was not explicitly addressed in sustainability and CSR reports.

Third, many of the retailers' approach to the SDGs may be seen to be driven
by cost savings, business efficiency drives and competitive pressures, as much as by

commitments to the SDGs and sustainable consumption. For example, in outlining its approach to "reducing energy intensity and emissions in our operations," Walmart (2017) argued that

> setting targets to cut greenhouse gas emissions in line with science is not just good for the planet, it's good for consumers and the bottom line. Walmart has sent a strong signal to other companies by shifting their business strategy to secure competitive advantage in the transition to a low-carbon economy.
>
> *(p. 53)*

Currently, amongst retailers, there is little evidence of widespread corporate or consumer appetite for a transition to a more sustainable future, which genuinely prioritises sustainable consumption, and such a scenario also seems currently politically unacceptable. However, it is important to recognise that retail changes do not take place within a vacuum and that while the leading retailers within the United Kingdom and the United States currently have the power to influence, and some critics would say, control, much of the environment in which they operate and trade, there are limits to their influence and power.

Conclusion

Retailers are the active intermediaries between primary producers and manufacturers on the one hand and consumers on the other, and as such can be seen to be in a singularly powerful position to play an important role in helping to achieve the SDGs. Many of the world's leading retailers have publicly reported on how they are looking to contribute to the SDGs. While some of them have emphasised that they will address all 17 SDGs, others initially plan to focus on a limited number. In both cases, the retailers have looked to align their commitment to the SDGs to their wider business strategies and sustainability programmes. However, the retailers' commitments to the SDGs are currently largely aspirational, some of them are focussed on domestic rather than international issues, and the retailers' role in achieving more sustainable patterns of SCP seems particularly challenging. As such, it remains to be seen how extensively leading retailers will be able to contribute to the achievement of the SDGs.

References

Aldi. (2018a). *Sustainable development goals*. Retrieved May 13, 2019, from https://cr.aldisouthgroup.com/en/cr-portal/simply-responsible/sustainable-development-goals

Aldi. (2018b). *Community*. Retrieved May 15, 2019, from https://cr.aldisouthgroup.com/en/cr-2017/community

Auchan. (2018). *CSR section of the 2017 management report*. Retrieved May 13, 2019, from www.auchan-holding.com/uploads/files/modules/downloads/1523966047_5ad5e05fc442b.pdf

British Retail Consortium. (2018). *Retail industry launches groundbreaking action plan to advance sustainability, development and equality*. Retrieved May 15, 2019, from https://brc.org.uk/news/2018/retail-industry-launches-ground-breaking-action-plan-to-advance-sustainability-development-and-equality

Durieu, X. (2003). How Europe's retail sector helps promote sustainable production. *Industry and Environment, 26*(1), 7–9.

European Commission. (2019). *Retail forum*. Retrieved May 11, 2019, from http://ec.europa.eu/environment/industry/retail/index_en.htm

Globe. (2014, March 26–28). *Sustainable consumption and retail – round table: Is sustainable retail an oxymoron? Thirteenth biennial conference and trade fair on business and the environment*. Conference Program. Vancouver, Canada. Retrieved May 15, 2019, from www.globeseries.com/forum2012/conference/conference-program/sustainable-consumption-retail.html

J. Sainsbury PLC. (2018). *Our values make us different: Sustainability update 2018*. Retrieved May 11, 2019, from www.about.sainsburys.co.uk/~/media/Files/S/Sainsburys/documents/making-a-difference/Sustainability_Update_2018.pdf

John Lewis & Partners. (2018a). *Sustainable development goals*. Retrieved May 11, 2019, from www.johnlewispartnership.co.uk/content/cws/csr/our-approach/sustainable-development-goals.html

John Lewis & Partners. (2018b). *Corporate responsibility report 2017–8*. Retrieved May 11, 2019, from www.johnlewispartnership.co.uk/content/dam/cws/pdfs/our-responsibilities/2018/jlp-cr-report-201718-digital.pdf

Jones, P., & Comfort, D. (2018). Sustainable consumption and the leading US retailers. *Indonesian Journal of CSR and Environmental Management, 1*(1). ISSN 2597-6192. Retrieved June 6, 2019, from http://eprints.glos.ac.uk/5342/2/5342%20Jones%20%282018%29%20Sustainable%20Consumption%20and%20the%20Leading%20US%20Retailers.pdf

Jones, P., Hillier, D., & Comfort, D. (2014). Sustainable consumption and the UK's leading retailers. *Social Responsibility Journal, 10*(4), 702–715.

Jones, P., Wynn, M., Comfort, D., & Hillier, D. (2007). CSR and UK retailers. *Issues in Social and Environmental Accounting, 1*(2), 243–258. Retrieved May 15, 2019, from http://eprints.glos.ac.uk/4267/1/CORPORATE%20SOCIAL%20RESPONSIBILITY%20AND%20UK%20RETAILERS.pdf

Kroger. (2018). *Kroger sustainability report 2018: Setting the table for a sustainable future*. Retrieved May 12, 2019, from http://sustainability.kroger.com/Kroger_CSR2018.pdf

Metro. (2018). *Responsibility: Corporate responsibility report 2017/18*. Retrieved June 20, 2019, from www.metroag.de/en/company/responsibility

Retail Industry Leaders Association. (2017). *Sustainability/environment*. Retrieved June 20, 2019, from www.rila.org/focus-areas/sustainability-environment

Rewe Group. (2018). *Rewe group sustainability report 2015–16*. Retrieved June 17, 2019, from https://rewe-group-nachhaltigkeitsbericht.de/2016/en/gri-report/management/gri-102-18-102-21-the-sustainability-strategy-of-rewe-group

Seven & I Holdings Co. (2018). *Corporate profile: Top message*. Retrieved September 17, 2018, from www.7andi.com/en/csr/greeting.html

Seyfang, G. (2004). *Local organic food: The social implications of sustainable consumption*. CSERGE Working Paper EDM, No. 04–09, the Centre for Social and Economic Research on the Global Environment, University of East Anglia. Retrieved June 17, 2019, from www.econstor.eu/bitstream/10419/80260/1/469899719.pdf

Target. (2018). *Future at heart: 2018 target corporate responsibility report*. Retrieved May 12, 2019, from https://corporate.target.com/_media/TargetCorp/csr/pdf/2018_corporate_responsibility_report.pdf

Tesco PLC. (2018). *Contributing to the UN sustainable development goals.* Retrieved May 12, 2019, from https://sustainability.tescoplc.com/media/475526/contributing-to-the-un-sustainable-development-goals_final.pdf

Walgreens Boots Alliance. (2017). *CSR report 2017.* Retrieved May 13, 2019, from www.walgreensbootsalliance.com/content/1110/files/Walgreens-Boots-Alliance-2017-Corporate-Social-Responsibility-Report.pdf

Walmart. (2017). *2017 global responsibility report.* Retrieved May 15, 2019, from https://cdn.corporate.walmart.com/95/08/2d1f094c430186c299788ac1935b/wmt-2017-grr-report-final.pdf

Walmart. (2018). *Business for 2030: Forging a path for business in the 2030 UN development agenda.* Retrieved May 11, 2019, from www.businessfor2030.org/walmart/

8

THE ENERGY INDUSTRY

Introduction

The World Bank (2018) reported that "the world is not on track to meet the global energy targets for 2030 set as part of the Sustainable Development Goals, but real progress is being made in certain areas" (para.1). Further, they concluded, "With the right approaches and policies, countries can make substantial progress in clean energy and energy access, and improve the lives of millions of people" (para.3). Nevertheless, Spencer Dale, BP's chief economist, in his analysis of energy supply and demand in 2018, notes, "Last year's developments sound yet another warning alarm that the world is on an unsustainable path" (BP, 2019, para.63) and that "what does seem fairly clear is that the underlying picture is one in which the actual pace of progress is falling well short of the accelerated transition envisaged by the Paris climate goals" (para.62). Against this backdrop, this chapter looks at a range of companies operating in the energy industry and examines how they are contributing to the SDGs and how they may do so in the future.

The companies reviewed here are from the different industry sectors that collectively make up the energy industry as a whole. They are E.ON, a UK gas and electricity supplier; Good Energy, a UK renewable energy supplier; BP, an international oil and gas exploration and production company; EDF Energy, the producer of one-fifth of the United Kingdom's electricity from its nuclear power stations, wind farms, coal- and gas-powered stations and combined heat and power plants; Drax Group, a UK electrical power generation company which runs Europe's biggest biomass-fuelled power station; Chevron, an American multinational energy corporation engaged in every aspect of the oil, natural gas and geothermal energy industries; Gazprom, a large Russian company, majority owned by the government of Russia, whose business is the extraction, production, transport and sale of natural gas; PetroChina, a state-owned Chinese oil and gas company; Shell, a British-Dutch oil and gas company headquartered in the Netherlands and incorporated in the United Kingdom; and ExxonMobil, the world's largest publicly traded international oil and gas company.

Overview of the energy industry and the SDGs

Most of the energy companies included in this study had a clear stance on the SDGs that they support (Table 8.1). For example, E.ON (2018) notes, "Our activities contribute in particular to the following goals: 7 – Ensuring that everyone has access to affordable, reliable, sustainable and modern forms of energy. . . (and) 13 – Immediately take action to combat climate change and its impacts" (para.1). In addition, "we are making a further contribution to the following SDGs" (para.1), and they then identify SDGs 3, 6, 9, 11 and 12. Similarly, Good Energy (2017) notes, "We've undertaken some early steps to identify which of the SDGs we can help deliver most. Not surprisingly, as a renewable energy company, our most direct contribution will be to Goal 7 on 'Clean and Affordable Energy' and Goal 13 on 'Climate Action'." They add, however that "we can deliver more on a wider set of Global Goals including those on Industry, Innovation and Infrastructure, Sustainable Cities and Communities, and Good Health and Wellbeing" (para.8).

TABLE 8.1 SDGs addressed by energy companies

SDG/ energy company	E.ON	BP	Good Energy	EDF	Drax	Chevron	Gazprom	Petro China	Shell	Exxon Mobil
1								x		x
2								x		
3	x		x	x		x	x	x		x
4				x		x	x	x		x
5				x			x	x		x
6	x	x				x	x	x		
7	x	x	x	x	x	x	x	x	x	x
8		x			x	x	x	x	x	x
9	x	x	x		x		x	x	x	
10				x				x		
11	x		x				x	x		
12	x	x		x			x	x	x	x
13	x	x	x	x	x	x	x	x	x	x
14		x		x			x	x		
15		x		x	x	x	x	x		
16								x		
17				x	x	x	x	x	x	

Drax Group (2018) asserts, "We are committed to play our part in achieving the UN SDGs through our operations, the services we deliver to our customers and in partnership with others" (para.1) and identifies SDGs 7, 8, 9, 13, 15, 17 as those where the company is particularly making progress. Royal Dutch Shell (Shell, 2017) identifies almost the exact same SDGs for their own support and progression. The company notes,

> We welcome the SDGs and we continue to develop our approach to how we can help achieve them. All the SDGs are relevant to Shell's operations to varying degrees and we are already contributing to many of these goals. In 2017, we prioritised six of the goals that have particular significance for Shell across our global business.
>
> *(para.3)*

These were SDGs 7, 8, 9, 12, 13 and 17 (Table 8.1). ExxonMobil (2018) also identifies SDGs 7 and 13 but also six others. They state, "While ExxonMobil contributes to certain aspects of all 17 SDGs, the following eight represent those most relevant to the company's sustainability focus areas" (para.5). The company identifies SDGs 1, 3, 4, 5, 7, 8, 12 and 13 as those they are actively progressing through.

The primary concentration on SDGs 7 and 13 is evident in many other energy industry reports and statements. BP (2017a), for example, states, "Our core business of delivering energy to the world contributes directly to goals 7, 8 and 13," but they also add "the way we operate supports the implementation of many of the other goals" (p. 78). These include SDGs 6, 9, 12, 14 and 15. Similarly, Chevron (2018) states that it is

> proud to contribute to the achievement of the SDGs. Our primary contribution is by safely developing and delivering affordable and reliable energy that is necessary for social and economic progress. We also contribute through our work in protecting people and the environment and by investing in health, education and economic development.
>
> *(para.2)*

The company identifies SDGs 7 and 13 for particular focus but also SDGs 3, 4, 6, 8, 15 and 17 (Table 8.1).

Other energy companies take a slightly different approach by stating their own sustainability goals and objectives and then linking them to particular SDGs. Gazprom (2017), for example, states

> The company's key sustainable development priorities are to maximize production safety, mitigate any environmental impacts, develop staff, promote the development of regions, and take stakeholders' interests into consideration. These priorities and their respective goals are consistent with global trends and sustainable development goals, in particular the sustainable development goals (SDGs) adopted by the UN in 2015.
>
> *(p. 40)*

The company then details its own goals and activities regarding the economy and manufacturing and suggests they are consistent with SDGs 8, 9 and 12; those concerning industrial safety align with SDGs 3, 6, 7, 13, 14 and 15; and its initiatives for social development support SDGs 4, 5, 8, 11 and 17.

EDF (2018) take a similar approach. The company has a "new strategic goal called Cap 2030: a responsible electricity company that champions low-carbon growth" (para 2), and

> we have adopted six Corporate Social Responsibility Goals, echoing the United Nations' 17 Sustainable Development Goals. Each reflects a strong climate and low-carbon commitment, human development of EDF Group's employees, offers for clients and especially the most vulnerable, energy efficiency, dialogue and consultation, and biodiversity conservation.
>
> *(para. 3)*

PetroChina claims to support all the SDGs. In its *2017 Sustainability Report* (PetroChina, 2017), the company links a range of SDGs to different aspects of their operations (Figure 8.1), but there is little detail on how they are pursuing them specifically.

 SUSTAINED ENERGY SUPPLY

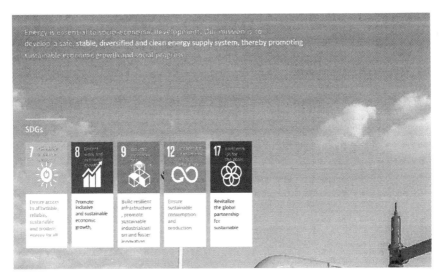

FIGURE 8.1 PetroChina links a range of SDGs to aspects of its mission, goals and operations

Source: PetroChina, 2017, p. 18.

Actions and activities regarding specific SDGs

As regards specific initiatives to support the SDGs, there are many examples of energy companies funding projects that, it can be said, are aligned with the SDGs. For example, as regards SDG3, Chevron (2017) notes,

> Working with partners, we support initiatives that build local capacity and deliver lasting gains in the fight against devastating diseases . . . we partner with Baylor College of Medicine International Pediatric AIDS Initiative at Texas Children's Hospital to provide training and health care to medically underserved populations in Africa and Latin America.
>
> *(p. 2)*

Regarding SDG6, Chevron (2017) claims, "Our operations promote the efficient use of water in water-constrained areas through conservation, reuse and recycling. In the Permian Basin, more than 95 percent of the water used in our well completions is from brackish water sources" (p. 2).

As regards more direct initiatives linked to their core energy operations, E.ON (2018) claims in the context of SDG7 that

> by expanding renewable energy and supporting our customers in their own production of clean electricity, we are contributing to a sustainable and climate-friendly energy supply. Our distribution grids are the platform connecting energy producers with consumers and play the key role in ensuring security of supply. We also offer assistance to economically disadvantaged customers – because energy should be equally available to all without interruption.
>
> *(para. 3)*

Chevron claims, to be

> a leader in supplying liquefied natural gas (LNG), a relatively lower-carbon-intensity fuel. Combined, our Gorgon and Wheatstone assets are expected to produce more than 24 million metric tons of LNG per year – enough to supply 16 percent of Japan's electricity and reduce GHG emissions from power generation by around 11 percent if used in lieu of coal.
>
> *(p. 2)*

Drax Group (2018) notes,

> We provide 6% of the UK's electricity and play a vital role in helping change the way energy is generated, supplied and used as the UK moves to a low-carbon future. In 2017, 65% of the electricity we produced came from biomass, rather than coal. Our B2B Energy Supply businesses encourage customers to

be more sustainable, including through the provision of reliable, renewable electricity at no premium compared to fossil fuel-generated electricity.

(para. 2)

BP (2017b) concede that "the world's rising demand for energy is a real opportunity to expand our business and deliver higher returns for our investors," but note "as we grow, our net operational emissions won't – and we will help others to curb their emissions. We will deliver this commitment by reducing emissions in our operations, improving our products and services, and creating low carbon businesses" (paras. 1/2). The company also claim (BP, 2017c) that "the energy we produce helps power economic growth and improve the quality of life for millions of people," citing as examples "countries from Brazil to Oman, and from the US to Indonesia" (paras. 1/2), where BP enables countries to "grow their domestic supplies of energy and boost their energy security. This, in turn, creates jobs, drives economic development and generates revenue for governments. The value we create can transform communities, even nations" (para. 4). For SDG8, Drax (2018) notes,

> We directly employ over 2,500 people in the United Kingdom and United States and their health, safety and wellbeing remains our highest priority. Our B2B Energy Supply business offers energy solutions and value-added services to industrial, corporate and small business customers across the UK
>
> *(para. 3)*

and Chevron (2017) comments that it is

> among Chevron's most powerful tools for creating prosperity are our supply chain and workforce investments. Much of Chevron's spending is on goods and services provided by locally owned companies. For example, in 2017, the Chevron-led Tengizchevroil joint venture spent more than $2.5 billion on Kazakhstani goods and services.
>
> *(p. 3)*

With regard to SDG12, BP (2017a) introduced a number of initiatives to limit emissions (Figure 8.2), noting, "We are playing our part by improving the efficiency of our existing operations and designing our new major projects to emit fewer greenhouse gases" (p. 13). They also note a range of related measures for tackling methane as a source of emissions, which "accounts for around 20% of manmade greenhouse gas emissions" (p. 15), "developing advanced fuels, lubricants and petrochemicals" (p. 26) and "carbon capture, use and storage" (p. 30). Regarding SDG13, Drax (2018) notes,

> Our electricity generation activities are a source of carbon emissions. We are committed to helping a low-carbon future by moving away from coal and towards renewable and cleaner fuels, including biomass electricity generation

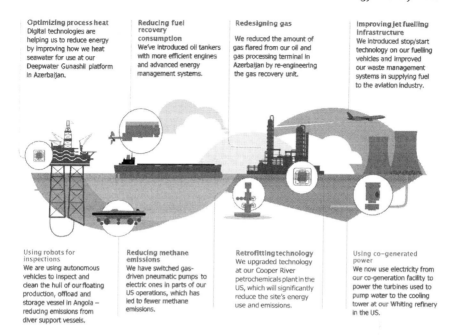

Optimizing process heat
Digital technologies are
helping us to reduce energy
by improving how we heat
seawater for use at our
Deepwater Gunashli platform
in Azerbaijan.

Reducing fuel
recovery
consumption
We've introduced oil tankers
with more efficient engines
and advanced energy
management systems.

Redesigning gas
We reduced the amount of
gas flared from our oil and
gas processing terminal in
Azerbaijan by re-engineering
the gas recovery unit.

Improving jet fuelling
infrastructure
We introduced stop/start
technology on our fuelling
vehicles and improved
our waste management
systems in supplying fuel
to the aviation industry.

Using robots for
inspections
We are using autonomous
vehicles to inspect and
clean the hull of our floating
production, offload and
storage vessel in Angola –
reducing emissions from
diver support vessels.

Reducing methane
emissions
We have switched gas-
driven pneumatic pumps to
electric ones in parts of our
US operations, which has
led to fewer methane
emissions.

Retrofitting technology
We upgraded technology
at our Cooper River
petrochemicals plant in the
US, which will significantly
reduce the site's energy
use and emissions.

Using co-generated
power
We now use electricity from
our co-generation facility to
power the turbines used to
pump water to the cooling
tower at our Whiting refinery
in the US.

FIGURE 8.2   BP's initiatives to limit emissions in support of SDG12

Source: BP, 2017a, p. 13.

and our planned rapid-response gas plants. We also help our business customers to be more sustainable through the supply of renewable electricity.

(para. 5)

Chevron is a founding partner of "the Environmental Partnership," a voluntary
industry initiative led by the American Petroleum Institute "with the goal of accelerating improvements to reduce methane and volatile organic compound emissions" (Chevron, 2017, p. 3).

Concerning SDG15, Chevron states,

We've been producing energy on Barrow Island for more than 50 years, and it
remains one of Australia's finest Class A Nature Reserves. We also promote and
protect biodiversity through our global social investments, such as our Maratua
Ecotourism for Sustainable Small Island program in East Kalimantan, Indonesia.

(p. 3)

Drax (2018) notes,

We source sustainable biomass for our electricity generation activities and
engage proactively with our supply chain to ensure that the forests we source
from are responsibly managed. We work closely with our suppliers and

through tough screening and audits ensure that we never cause deforestation, forest decline or source from areas officially protected from forestry activities or where endangered species may be harmed.

(para. 6)

For SDG17, Chevron (2017) claims, "Our partnership initiatives around the world strengthen local economies through programs that provide microloan services, support enterprise and workforce development, and improve education. Among these are the Niger Delta, Appalachia, Bangladesh and Thailand partnership initiatives" (p. 3). Drax (2018) states, "We engage with stakeholders regularly and build relationships with partners to raise our standards and maximise what can be achieved. Our collaborations align closely with our business, purpose and strategy" (para.7).

Discussion

The earlier examples of energy companies' attitudes and approaches to the SDGs raises a number of issues. First, the energy industry is in a unique position to contribute to the SDGs. Its core business is central to a number of the SDGs and the industry can make a significant contribution to their implementation; but it is also not difficult to allude to these goals with empty rhetoric. This last point is borne out by some of the material cited earlier. A number of companies link their ongoing activities to the SDGs without specifying how they will make any significant impact. This is recognised by Good Energy (2017) when they conclude, "To really make a difference, this has to be much more than a tick box exercise" (para. 9). In the case of Good Energy, this led them to

use the Goals as a framework for the evolution of the Good Energy brand and to guide formal decision-making in the business. If we're considering doing something new or different, the Goals can be a helpful reference point. And we're already testing the Goals as a framework for external reporting, for example as part of our most recent annual report to the Social Stock Exchange.

(para. 9)

The need to go beyond a mere tick-box exercise is a key theme that emerges from the previous industry examples.

Second, governments need to establish and apply appropriate policies and incentives to encourage energy companies, and the public at large, to progress the SDGs concerning energy production and consumption. The United Nations and KPMG (2017) in their "SDG Industry Matrix for Energy, Natural Resources and Chemicals" note that, "the SDGs can only be achieved with involvement of the private sector working alongside Governments, Parliaments, the UN system and other international institutions" (p. 2). In this context, BP (2017d), for example, asserts,

We believe that carbon pricing is the most effective way to incentivize everyone – energy producers and consumers alike – to play their part in reducing emissions. It makes energy efficiency more attractive and low carbon solutions, such as renewables and carbon capture, use and storage (CCUS), more cost competitive . . . we believe CCUS has a vital role to play in meeting the objectives of the Paris Agreement. It can achieve deep emissions reductions in existing power infrastructure and energy-intensive industries that rely on the use of fossil fuels. The technology has been in use for more than 20 years, but needs governmental support – through a carbon price and other policy measures – to accelerate its deployment.

(p. 23)

Third, and related to the aforementioned, there is a need for cross-industry collaboration with appropriate involvement from government agencies. Shell (2017) notes that "governments are responsible for prioritising and implementing approaches that meet the SDGs. But achieving these tasks will require collaboration between civil society, governments, the private sector, non-governmental organisations and the public" (para.3). In recognition of the problems of effective and coordinated action from the industry, Shell (2017) notes,

Through IPIECA, the global oil and gas industry association for environmental and social issues, we have collaborated with the UN Development Programme and the World Bank's International Finance Corporation, to develop a shared understanding of how our industry can most effectively support the goals.

(para. 3)

This resulted in the publication *Mapping the Oil and Gas Industry to the Sustainable Development Goals: An Atlas* (IPIECA, UNDP, & IFC, 2017a). This document discusses the links between the oil and gas industry, "maps the industry's existing contributions and encourages companies to identify additional opportunities to help countries progress towards the Goals," and can "assist oil and gas companies and their stakeholders in developing a shared understanding of how the industry manages environmental and social challenges while maximizing economic benefits" (p. 1).

The *Atlas* aims to facilitate three main outcomes – first, an "enhanced understanding of the relationship between the SDGs and the oil and gas industry"; second, an "increased awareness of the opportunities and challenges that the SDGs pose for the oil and gas industry and its stakeholders, and the ways in which the industry might address them"; and third, the advancement of "multistakeholder dialogue and collaboration towards enhancing the contribution of the oil and gas sector to the achievement of the SDGs" (IPIECA, UNDP, & IFC, 2017a, p. 1). The *Atlas* identifies eight of the goals "where the industry typically can make important contributions" (p. 2). These are SDGs 3, 6, 7, 8, 9, 13, 14 and 15, which align very closely with the goals highlighted in the company reports, as depicted in Table 8.1. However, for all 17 SDGs, the *Atlas* provides a set of "key issue areas," which it divides into two camps – those that will help "Integrate (the SDGs) into Core Business" and those that will help "Collaborate and Leverage" (p. 3).

Conclusion

All the energy companies reviewed in this chapter claim to be making positive moves in support of some or all of the SDGs. They all identified SDG7 and SDG13 as SDGs where they were making a particular impact and this is supported by cross-industry initiatives (IPIECA, UNDP, & IFC, 2017a). The energy industry is in a unique position to have a major impact in the achievement of these and other of the SDGs, but there will inevitably be some tensions between immediate shareholder value and more altruistic aspirations. It is also easy for companies to state their alignment to certain SDGs, but there may be discrepancies between stated intent, action and impact.

It is, nevertheless, encouraging that the World Bank (2018) report that "real progress is being made in certain areas – particularly expansion of access to electricity in least developed countries, and industrial energy efficiency" (para.1) and "renewable energy is making impressive gains in the electricity sector" (para.2). However, they also note "these are not being matched in transportation and heating – which together account for 80% of global energy consumption" (para.2). The need for government action and cross-industry initiatives is paramount. This is reinforced by BP (2017d), which, in the context of climate change, concludes, "No one company or sector alone can deliver a low carbon future. Everyone, from consumers to corporations to governments, needs to take responsibility. If we respond collectively, even a challenge as complex as climate change can be met" (p. 24).

References

BP. (2017a). *BP sustainability report 2017 – how will BP respond to global change.* Retrieved November 30, 2018, from www.bp.com/content/dam/bp/en/corporate/pdf/sustainability-report/group-reports/bp-sustainability-report-2017.pdf

BP. (2017b). *Sustainability advancing low carbon.* Retrieved October 8, 2019, from https://www.bp.com/en/global/bp-petrochemicals/sustainability.html

BP. (2017c). *Value to society.* Retrieved January 13, 2019, from www.bp.com/en/global/corporate/sustainability/value-to-society.html

BP. (2017d). *Advancing the energy transition.* Retrieved January 13, 2019, from www.bp.com/en/global/corporate/sustainability/climate-change.html

BP. (2019). *Energy in 2018: An unsustainable path.* Retrieved June 20, 2019, from www.bp.com/en/global/corporate/energy-economics/statistical-review-of-world-energy/chief-economist-analysis.html

Chevron. (2017). *2017 corporate responsibility report highlights.* Retrieved December 1, 2018, from www.chevron.com/-/media/shared-media/documents/2017-corporate-responsibility-report.pdf

Chevron. (2018). *Chevron and the UN SDGs: The business of progress.* Retrieved December 1, 2018, from www.chevron.com/-/media/chevron/PDF-Reports/stories/chevron-and-the-u-n-sustainable-development-goals.pdf

Drax. (2018). *The sustainable development goals.* Retrieved November 30, 2018, from www.drax.com/sustainability/sustainable-development-goals/

EDF. (2018). *Our six corporate social responsibility goals.* Retrieved November 30, 2018, from www.edf.fr/en/the-edf-group/our-commitments/corporate-social-responsibility

E.ON. (2018). *Our contribution to SDGs.* Retrieved October 16, 2018, from www.eon.com/ en/about-us/sustainability/sustainability-development.html

Gazprom. (2017). *Aiming higher – 2017 sustainable development report.* Retrieved June 20, 2017, from www.gazprom-neft.com/annual-reports/2017/GPN_CSR2017_ENG_200718.pdf

Good Energy. (2017). *Sustainable development goals – why should businesses care?* Retrieved November 29, 2018, from www.goodenergy.co.uk/blog/2017/04/18/sustainable-development-goals/

IPIECA, UNDP, & IFC. (2017a). *Mapping the oil and gas industry to the sustainable development goals: An atlas.* Retrieved January 21, 2019, from www.ipieca.org/resources/awareness-briefing/ mapping-the-oil-and-gas-industry-to-the-sustainable-development-goals-an-atlas/

PetroChina. (2017). *Sustainability report 2017.* Retrieved January 20, 2019, from www.petro china.com.cn/petrochina/xhtml/images/shyhj/2017kcxfzbgen.pdf

Shell. (2017). *Sustainability report 2017.* Retrieved December 6, 2018, from http://reports. shell.com/sustainability-report/2017/our-contribution-to-society/sustainable-develop ment-goals.html

United Nations and KPMG. (2017). *SDG industry matrix: Energy, natural resources and chemicals.* Retrieved June 17, 2019, from https://home.kpmg/content/dam/kpmg/xx/ pdf/2017/05/sdg-energy.pdf

World Bank. (2018, May 2). *Progress on global energy goals slow, but strong gains in countries show promise.* Press Release. Retrieved December 1, 2018, from www.worldbank.org/en/news/ press-release/2018/05/02/sustainable-development-goal-sdg-7-global-progress-report

9

CONCLUSION

Introduction

Within the main body of this text, the authors have explored how leading companies within a range of business sectors are looking to contribute to the achievement of the SDGs. The aim of this concluding chapter is to provide an overview of the findings from the eight industry sectors studied and to address the original research questions. This involves consideration of a range of issues and challenges facing business enterprises in supporting the SDGs and contributing to sustainable development.

After this introductory section, the three research questions (RQs) noted in the introduction to this book are addressed. They are:

- How have different industry sectors responded to the challenges set by the SDGs?
- What are the key themes arising from the varying approaches to the SDGs adopted by different industry sectors?
- What are the critical issues for the continued support and delivery of the SDGs?

RQ1: How have different industry sectors responded to the challenges set by the SDGs?

The most supported SDGs across all eight industry sectors were SDGs 13, 8 and 12, and the least favoured were SDGs 1, 16, 2 and 14 (Table 9.1). Eighty-five percent of all companies supported SDG13, 71% supported SDG8 and 70% supported SDG12. At the other end of the spectrum, only 30% or less of all companies supported SDGs 1, 2 and 16 (Table 9.2). The bottom row in Table 9.1 indicates the average number of SDGs supported in each industry sector by each company. Only in the retail industry were more than a third of the 17 SDGs supported, on average, by the ten organisations reviewed. After retail, the most supportive industry sectors were pharmaceuticals and energy; the least supportive, by this measure, were the marketing and media and the automobile industries.

These findings, which align closely with those of the study of the G250 companies by KPMG (KPMG, 2018), illustrate a number of key points. The widespread support for SDG13 reflects the global concern for the impact of climate change. As was noted at the United Nations Framework Convention on Climate Change (2018), "Climate change presents the single biggest threat to sustainable development everywhere and its widespread, unprecedented impacts disproportionately burden the poorest and most vulnerable" (para.1), and thus "urgent action to halt climate change and deal with its impacts is integral to the successful implementation of the SDGs" (para.2). Pharmaceutical company GSK (2016) also remarked, "Climate change is one of the world's most pressing issues and a major threat to people's health and global economic development" (p. 2). The next most supported SDGs were SDGs 8 and 12, and this arguably reflects what is deemed most within the scope of private-sector operations. Equally, those SDGs concerning poverty, peace and justice and hunger were the least well supported. Whilst this is regrettable and could be seen as a sad comment on the business environment, it is understandable in terms of stakeholder priorities and what is considered realistically achievable.

TABLE 9.1 SDG support across the eight industry sectors studied

SDG/ sector	Financial services	ICT	Automobile	Hotel	Marketing and media	Pharmaceuticals	Retail	Energy	Average by SDG
1	6	4	1	2	1	2	3	2	2.6
2	3	4	1	2	2	3	8	1	3.0
3	6	5	7	5	5	10	7	7	6.4
4	6	7	3	3	3	6	3	5	4.5
5	7	6	3	4	6	10	6	4	5.7
6	4	4	4	5	3	7	6	5	4.7
7	8	4	4	2	2	5	6	10	5.0
8	8	7	5	10	4	6	10	7	7.1
9	7	6	5	2	1	6	3	7	4.6
10	5	4	2	7	4	2	4	2	3.7
11	8	7	7	4	0	1	5	4	4.6
12	6	5	7	8	6	8	10	7	7.0
13	10	9	10	9	5	7	8	10	8.5
14	3	3	1	4	1	1	8	4	3.1
15	4	4	1	4	1	2	7	6	3.6
16	3	3	2	3	3	5	4	1	3.0
17	4	3	1	5	4	9	4	6	4.5
Average by sector	5.8	5.0	3.8	4.6	2.9	5.3	6.0	5.2	

While some major companies within each of the selected business sectors claimed to be addressing all 17 SDGs, many have chosen to target a number of specific SDGs that they feel are aligned with their corporate goals and business strategies and where they feel they can make the most valuable contribution to the SDGs. Many of the energy companies, for example, identified SDGs 7 and 13 for their primary focus, and these two goals were supported in some measure by all ten energy companies in the study. As BP (2017), commented, "Our core business of delivering energy to the world contributes directly to goals 7, 8 and 13" (p. 78). All ten companies in the automobile sector also supported SDG13. In the pharmaceutical industry, all ten companies supported SDG3. Johnson & Johnson (2019), for example, noted, "We are dedicating our expertise, ideas and ingenuity to catalyze efforts toward achieving SDG3, Good Health and Well-being, which is at the heart of the Sustainable Development Goals and the core of our business" (para.5). In the retail sector, SDG12 received support from all ten companies, as did SDG8.

TABLE 9.2 Percentage of companies and organisations supporting each SDG

SDG	% Goal
13	85 Take urgent action to combat **climate change** and its impacts
8	71 Promote sustained, inclusive and sustainable **economic growth**, full and productive **employment** and decent work for all
12	70 Ensure sustainable **consumption and production** patterns
3	64 Ensure healthy lives and promote **well-being** for all at all ages
5	57 Achieve **gender equality** and empower all women and girls
7	50 Ensure access to affordable, reliable, sustainable and modern **energy** for all
6	47 Ensure availability and sustainable management of **water and sanitation** for all
9	46 Build resilient **infrastructure**, promote inclusive and sustainable industrialisation and foster innovation
11	46 Make **cities and human settlements** inclusive, safe, resilient and sustainable
17	45 Strengthen the means of implementation and revitalise the **global partnership** for sustainable development
4	45 Ensure inclusive and equitable quality education and promote lifelong learning opportunities for all
10	37 Reduce **inequality** within and amongst countries
15	36 Protect, restore and promote sustainable use of **terrestrial ecosystems**, sustainably manage forests, combat desertification, and halt and reverse land degradation and halt biodiversity loss
14	31 Conserve and sustainably use the **oceans, seas and marine resources** for sustainable development
2	30 End **hunger**, achieve food security and improved nutrition and promote . . . sustainable agriculture
16	30 Promote **peaceful and inclusive societies** for sustainable development, provide access to justice for all and build effective, accountable and inclusive institutions at all levels
1	26 End **poverty** in all its forms everywhere

Many companies did not explicitly address the SDGs *per se* but rather claimed to have aligned their sustainability goals to the SDGs, or to have integrated the SDGs into their business or sustainability strategies. Within UK retailing, John Lewis & Partners (2018) identified nine SDGs as their priorities and emphasised that these priorities are aligned with a number of its corporate goals, which look, for example, to "source and sell with integrity," "unlock partner potential" and "deliver more with less" (p. 26). The marketing company Publicis chose to focus its energies on ten of the SDGs, noting, "Our approach is pragmatic and directly linked to social, societal and environmental responsibilities that are already part of our Groupe strategy" (Publicis, 2018, para.2). The Hyatt Hotel Corporation (2018) noted, "Our corporate responsibility work supports the mission of the UN SDGs" (para.5). The company's corporate responsibility strategy embraces six key sets of issues – namely, "our people," "our communities," "human rights," "our planet," "responsible sourcing" and "responsible seafood" (para.2), and each of these sets of issues is aligned to a number of the SDGs. In a similar vein, Hewlett-Packard (2017) "supports the United Nations Sustainable Development Goals, and remains committed to driving progress on selected goals that are closely aligned to our Sustainable Impact strategy" (p. 26). Meliá Hotels matched the SDGs with the goals of its own CSR model to "align Company goals with the universal goals inspired by the United Nations" (Meliá Hotels International, 2016, para.5).

In some instances, this process of alignment is more general, and the link to the specific SDGs and targets is less clear. Fujitsu (2018) suggested, "The SDGs are one element in an ecosystem aimed at achieving the Fujitsu growth strategy of 'connected services', pointing the way to new business opportunities through ventures that work to resolve social issues" (para.3). Toshiba (2018) noted, "Our Carbon Zero programme supports 13 of the 17 Sustainable Development Goals set by the UN" (para.1), and BNP Paribas claimed to "have mapped our entire business to the UN's SDGs" (BNP Paribas, 2019, para.10). AXA (2017) claimed that "through its activities, investments and strategic focus," the company "is a responsible actor and responsible to its environment" and that all its "responsible actions are aligned with the UN SDGs" (p. 47).

RQ2: What are the key themes arising from the varying approaches to the SDGs adopted by different industry sectors?

The sustainability concept and shared value

The varied support for specific SDGs noted earlier is undoubtedly related to the business community's conception of sustainability, which generally tends to emphasise business continuity, business efficiency and cost savings, as well as the principles underpinning the SDGs. Thus while many of the environmental agendas addressed by the selected companies are designed to reduce carbon dioxide emissions and to increase energy efficiency, for example, they also serve to reduce operating costs. In a similar vein, the selected companies' commitments to their employees, focusing on, for example, empowering employees and health and safety, also help to promote stability, security, loyalty and efficiency amongst the workforce.

Porter and Kramer (2011) defined the concept of shared value as "corporate policies and practices that enhance the competitiveness of the company while simultaneously advancing social and economic conditions in the communities in which it sells and operates" (p. 2), and in many ways, this represents the approaches of the companies studied here to sustainability and the SDGs. Indeed, the concept has been increasingly adopted by a small, but growing, group of large companies. Nestle (2017a), for example, claimed,

> Creating Shared Value (CSV) is fundamental to how we do business at Nestlé. We believe that our company will be successful in the long term by creating value for both our shareholders and for society. Our activities and products should make a positive difference to society while contributing to Nestlé's ongoing success.
>
> *(para. 1)*

The company also noted

> linking the SDGs with CSV and our material issues helped us look more closely at where we can have the biggest impact. Today, our sustainability strategy is carefully mapped against the 17 goals, with each commitment and impact area corresponding to one or more of them.
>
> *(Nestle, 2017b, para. 3)*

Similarly, as noted in Chapter 3, Volvo Group (2017), stated, "Creating shared value involves moving both our business and society forward. We enhance our competitiveness while simultaneously advancing the economic, environmental and social conditions of the societies in which we operate" (p. 78).

Crane, Palazzo, Spence and Matten (2014), however, identified a number of weaknesses and shortcomings in the shared value model. More specifically, they argued that the model "ignores the tensions between social and economic goals," that it is "naïve about the challenges of business compliance" and that it is "based on a shallow conception of the corporation's role in society" (p. 130). In examining the first of these concerns, the authors suggested that "many corporate decisions related to social and environmental problems, however creative the decision maker may be, do not present themselves as potential win–wins, but rather manifest themselves in terms of dilemmas" (p. 136). The authors maintained that such dilemmas are effectively "continuous struggles between corporations and their stakeholders over limited resources and recognition" (p. 136).

Nevertheless, Citibank (2017) provides a good example of how the alignment of company objectives with some of the SDGs can be seen to deliver shared value. The bank states,

> We are well-positioned to contribute to several of the SDGs. The energy and climate goals (SDGs 7 and 13), for example, are aligned with our progress toward our $100billion Environmental Finance and operational footprint goals. Improving cities continues to be a central tenet of our work and is also central to the resilient infrastructure and sustainable cities goals (SDGs 9 and 11). Promoting economic progress – the emphasis of another one of the goals (SDG 8) – ties directly to our efforts to boost economic and job growth. Gender equality (SDG 5) is also a focus of our engagement efforts, both with our own workforce and in the communities that we support. And we do all of this work through partnerships (SDG 17) with our clients and other stakeholders.
>
> *(p. 7)*

Reporting and materiality

Corporate sustainability has become an increasingly important business imperative, and if companies are to contribute meaningfully to the SDGs, they will certainly need to integrate their achievements into their reporting processes. KPMG (2011), for example, argued, "Companies are increasingly realizing that corporate responsibility reporting is about more than just being a good corporate citizen; it drives innovation and promotes learning, which helps companies grow their business and increases their organization's value" (p. 2). In a similar vein, the Global Reporting Initiative (2013) suggests that sustainability reporting "encourages good management and serves as an incentive for the establishment of a culture of corporate transparency" (p. 4). If sustainability reporting is to achieve these goals, then it is vitally important that companies publishing corporate sustainability reports address the issues of materiality and independent external assurance. Even in 2018, however, KPMG (2018) reported that "there is not yet an established process, benchmark or standard for reporting on the SDGs, even though many organisations are developing tools and communities to help companies respond" (p. 2).

Nevertheless, there are examples from the companies studied of clear reporting against targets. Nissan (2018), for example, has specified its own approach, its own indicators and its own targets in support of several SDGs, and it has measured its performance against these (Table 3.2). This raises the issue of "materiality" or "material issues," which the Global Reporting Initiative (2014) defines as "those topics that have a direct or indirect impact on an organization's ability to create, preserve or erode economic, environmental and social value for itself, its stakeholders and society at large" (para.2). The concept of materiality can be traced to the auditing and accounting processes associated with traditional financial reporting, but it is increasingly seen to be vitally important in sustainability reporting, and there is some consensus that it includes a wider range of issues and actions than financial reporting.

The ways in which companies have identified and operationalised materiality in their sustainability reporting processes varies widely, but several of the companies studied here have included the pursuit of the SDGs to their CSR reports. Mitsubishi (2018), rather like Nissan, "has specified CSR materiality and defined individual targets and KPIs, and is pushing ahead with initiatives to achieve the targets." The company adds that it "will specify and revise our CSR materiality with a focus on how we can contribute to resolving social issues as a company, and seek to contribute to realizing the SDGs through the initiatives we apply to the CSR materiality" (para.9). In the automobile industry, the latest sustainability report from the Society of Motor Manufacturers and Traders (2018) includes a materiality assessment (see Figure 3.1) for the first time. The majority of issues identified as being of high importance to the automotive industry and to external stakeholders align with one or the other of the SDGs. Nevertheless, more generally, there is little indication to date of how such a process has informed companies' selection of their priorities for sustainability.

More specifically, the Governance and Accountability Institute (2014), in their study of 1,246 organisations, emphasised how the process of determining materiality varied from sector to sector and from company to company. This is borne out by the unanimous support of the energy companies for SDGs 7 and 13, and that of the pharmaceutical companies for SDG3. In arguing the case for "sector specific materiality and sustainability reporting standards" Eccles, Krzus, Rogers and Serafeim (2012) have stated, "Without standards it is difficult for companies to know exactly how to measure and report on some dimensions of sustainability performance" and to make "comparisons of performance among companies and over time" (p. 8). The authors further suggested that while "not a panacea," the development of "sector specific guidelines on what sustainability issues are material to that sector and the key performance indicators for reporting on them would significantly improve the ability of companies to report on their environmental, social and governance performance" (p. 13). They conclude that a company's failure to disclose material information in a comparable format has two downsides – namely, "companies are not adequately managing important business issues" and "risk to investors' portfolios, such as exposure to climate change, remain hidden" (p. 14). More recently, Eccles (2018) has noted, "Material environmental, social, and governance (ESG) issues . . . vary by industry (e.g., access to medicine is material for a pharmaceutical company but irrelevant to a chemical company where carbon emissions is material)," and, therefore, "it follows that any given industry will be more important to some SDGs than others" (paras.1 and 2).

Metrics and measurement

There are a number of issues about metrics and measurement relating to the SDGs, and Future Earth (2015) stressed the need for clear measurable targets. PWC (2017), in the context of assessing performance against the SDGs, questioned whether companies were "simply paying lip service to the goals they aspired to address or were they making tangible progress that they could measure, account for and report on?" (p. 4). More critically, Liverman (2018) claimed, "The expansion in the number of goals and targets, especially as indicators are developed for measuring progress towards targets, will add even more calculation, monitoring and quantification to the process." Further, she adds, "This is evident in the many calls to take advantage of new technologies – remote sensing, social media, big data analysis – for creating social and environmental indicators" (p. 178). This in turn led her to claim, "This can result in overly narrow assessments that direct policy towards quantifiable outcomes rather than broader but harder to measure social needs" (p. 178). Moseley (2018) also questioned "the value of engaging with development metrics" and suggested this was akin to "walking into an intellectual cul-de-sac of sorts, a debate where the parameters are too restrictively defined" (p. 201) and that the SDGs were deficient in what they measure and do not measure.

Nevertheless, several of the companies studied are attempting to confront these issues. In the finance sector, for example, Standard Chartered Bank (2019) reported that "our sustainability aspirations build on our three sustainability pillars with measurable targets to demonstrate how we are achieving sustainable outcomes across our business" and that "these also allow us to measure our contribution to the United Nations Sustainable Development Goals" (p. 1). The company's three pillars are "contributing to sustainable economic growth," "being a responsible company" and "investing in communities." Many of the companies studied have clear targets for reductions in carbon emissions, water usage and waste. Marriott International Hotels, for example, has committed to reducing water use by 15%, carbon emissions by 30%, waste by 45% and food waste by 50%, all by 2025. Kroger (2018) aims "to achieve zero waste in our operations by 2020 (and), zero food waste across our company by 2025" (p. 24). BNP Paribas (2019) "set science-based targets for ourselves to reduce our carbon footprint towards the 1.5C scenario – the globally agreed level at which to limit temperature rise to curb global warming" (para.7), and Vodafone (2018) notes, as their objectives regarding SDG13, a willingness "to reduce our greenhouse gas emissions by 40%; to purchase 100% of the electricity we use from renewable sources" (p. 3).

More generally, the dominant approach to the measurement and monitoring of the SDGs is to identify indicators for each SDG, but Bali Swain (2018) argued that this approach is inadequate, not least in that it ignores the complex interrelationships between some of the SDGs. At the same time, the United Nations Division for Sustainable Development Goals (2018) acknowledged that many important issues cut across goals and targets and that the goals and targets are themselves interdependent, and they must, therefore, be pursued together since progress in one area often depends on progress in other areas. It was emphasised, for example, "that ending poverty must go hand-in-hand with strategies that build economic growth and address a range of social needs including education, health, equality and job opportunities, while tackling climate change and working to preserve our ocean and forests" (para.1). This was recognised by Sabia Schwarzer, head of Group Communications and Corporate Responsibility at Allianz SE. She notes,

> Given the nature and size of our business, we have the opportunity to impact many of the targets set by the SDGs. However, one of the complexities of the

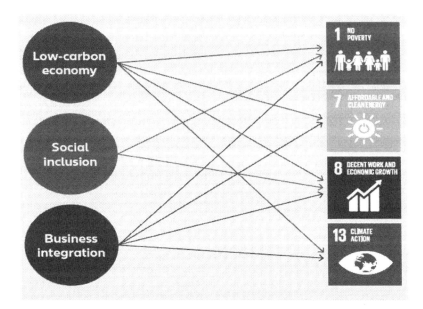

FIGURE 9.1 How Allianz's three strategic pillars align with the SDGs

Source: Allianz, 2017, p. 9.

> SDGs is their interconnectedness. You cannot single out one or two goals to which you solely contribute. In addition, our business activities and relationships are interconnected as well, which makes impact measurement challenging, be it positive or negative.
>
> *(Allianz, 2017, p. 9)*

In an attempt to address this issue, Allianz identified the multiple links between their "strategic pillars" and related SDGs (Figure 9.1), and between their own targets and the related SDG targets (Table 9.3). Similarly, pharmaceutical company MSD (2018) identified from the 169 UN targets, "11 targets for our priority SDGs that most closely align with our business" (para.8), and further, "we have identified existing metrics that enable us to quantitatively demonstrate our progress in support of the global goals" (para.7).

RQ3: What are the critical issues for the continued support and delivery of the SDGs?

The role of governments

In June 2019, the United Kingdom became the first country to announce that greenhouse gas emissions will be cut to almost zero by 2050 under the terms of a new government plan to tackle climate change. The potential implications of this

TABLE 9.3 Allianz's low-carbon economy pillar: links between company targets and achievements and the SDG targets

Low-carbon economy

Targets	Target-SDG link	Achievements in 2017
• Increase debt and equity investments in renewable energy in the mid-term	7.1, 7.2	• One billion euro new debt and equity investments in renewable energy in 2017, with a total of 5.6 billion euro
• 30% reduction of CO_2 emissions per employee by 2020 (2010 baseline)	13.2	• Divestment of 40 million euro in equities from coal-based business models (total to date: 265 million euro); run-off
• 30% reduction in energy consumption per employee by 2020 (2010 baseline)	13.2, 12.2	of 0.9 billion Euro in fixed income investments (total to date: 4.8 billion euro)
• 40% paper reduction by 2020 (2014 baseline)	13.2, 12.2	• We retired 425,367 carbon credits • Launched systematic approach for engagement with investee companies on ESG grounds
• Further investigate a more holistic role of green energy in our operations		• 165 Sustainable Solutions generated 121 billion euro in revenue • Reduced CO_2 emissions by 17% per employee against our 2010 baseline • 29% cut in energy consumption from office buildings per employee against our 2010 baseline • 40% of the energy we used came from renewable, low-carbon sources • Achieved a 27% paper reduction per employee against our 2014 baseline • The scope of our EMS included 91.1% of employees

Source: Allianz, 2017, p. 76.

intervention accord with the need for partnerships – and particularly those involving national governments – which many of the companies involved in this study have stressed. Industry has frequently emphasised its own commitment to contributing to the achievement of the SDGs, but it has also argued that governments have a vital enabling role in allowing the private sector to make that contribution. For example, Dell (2017) noted that the company "expects major SDG initiatives to be driven primarily at governmental or intergovernmental levels . . . governmental efforts will frequently need to partner or collaborate with the commercial sector in order to have maximum effect" (p. 2). Ericsson and the Earth Institute Columbia University (2016) also argued that "fulfilling the SDGs calls for multi-sectoral partnerships" and that "many of the challenges of sustainable development – health, education, infrastructure and environmental sustainability – require a deep role for policy makers and the public sector to drive progress by 2030" (p. 16), and Shell

(2017) asserted that "governments are responsible for prioritising and implementing approaches that meet the SDGs. But achieving these tasks will require collaboration between civil society, governments, the private sector, non-governmental organisations and the public" (para.3). GeSI (2016) similarly suggested that "the hurdles the world needs to clear . . . to meet the UN's ambitious deadline for achieving the SDGs" (p. 33) included political and regulatory blockages, and called on "the private sector and policy makers alike" to create the needed environment to "further sustainable development" (p. 35).

The UN itself have consistently emphasised that "governments play a key role in achieving the development goals and targets" (United Nations Department of Economic and Social Affairs, 2015, para.3). Whilst there is widespread support for this perspective, it is also clear that this is a complex issue. The OECD (2017), for example, has noted, "Multiplying the complex equation of complementarities and trade-offs across the whole spectrum of policy areas covered by the SDGs implies a need for prioritisation and negotiation involving all parts of government as well as the business sector and civil society." The OECD (2017) concluded that "in short: delivering on the SDGs is a formidable governance challenge – irrespective of countries' income levels" (p. 3).

The need for strategic prioritisation

Current business approaches to prioritising the SDGs have been called into question. A survey carried out by PWC (2018), for example, concluded that

> many companies are engaging at a more superficial level, showing that they are still struggling to identify how and why individual SDGs are relevant to their business. As a result, they are failing both to prioritise goals that need corporate support the most, and to address those that could cause them the biggest problems in the future if left unchecked.
>
> *(para. 2)*

The survey findings suggested that prioritising the SDGs "requires an understanding of the particular issues at a country or local level, combined with an analysis of business operations, and sourcing and supply chain" (para.9). At the same time, PWC argued that prioritisation

> also requires a longer-term vision of, and approach to, business growth strategy and planning than some companies are used to employing. To have that longer term perspective requires an understanding of the risks they face if underlying SDG issues are not solved, as well as available opportunities from adapting products and services towards innovations and solutions."
>
> *(para. 9)*

Moseley (2018) also suggested that there is little evidence of the strategic prioritisation of the SDGs within the business community.

Nevertheless, some of the companies in this study are using a materiality matrix to help develop such a strategic prioritisation. IHG (2018), for example, noted,

> We use a materiality matrix to embed our responsible business priorities with IHG's strategic approach and our principal risks. We consider the areas where we can make the greatest positive contribution and the matrix, together with stakeholder feedback, helps us identify our responsible business targets.
>
> *(p. 7)*

The company identifies a range of issues classified under their "three key pillars: our culture; our hotels; and our communities" (p. 3) and ranks their importance to both the company and their stakeholders (Figure 9.2).

This is a rapidly evolving situation, as companies come to terms with the pressures and opportunities relating to incorporation of the SDGs within their broader business strategies. This is evidenced by the change in approach by ITV over the past 15 years. In 2004, ITV (2004) noted

> corporate responsibility (CR) is a broad field that invites diverse views from a wide range of people. To make CR meaningful to our business it is essential to be clear about our view of the priorities for ITV. We base these on an assessment of what is material to our business. We identify material issues by considering the potential for an issue to impact on our business in the short and medium term. This will normally be by influencing our relationships and reputation with the stakeholder groups key to our business success.
>
> *(p. 2)*

However, by 2017, the company noted, "Our CR Strategy supports the delivery of ITV's strategy and priorities by seeking to manage risks to the business and maximise opportunities" and added "our CR Strategy focuses on three priorities: People, Planet and Partnerships. These three pillars are underpinned by core responsible business practices such as good governance, business ethics, data protection, responsibility of content and performance management" (ITV, 2017, p. 2). Many companies are now linking their CSR reporting into their overall business strategies. The challenge now is to bring their support for the SDGs fully within this debate and corporate strategy.

Vodafone (2018) illustrate how companies are moving to adopt a more strategic approach to their support for the SDGs. The company states "our sustainable business strategy sets out our commitment to maximise the social and economic benefits our business can deliver, while enhancing our commitment to responsible behaviour and corporate transparency" (p. 3). "Vodafone's strategy focuses on five SDGs. Through the impact of our extensive global network,

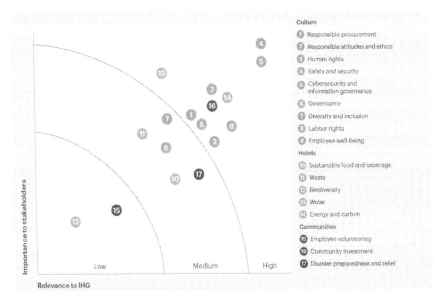

FIGURE 9.2 IHG's materiality matrix

Source: IHG, 2018, p. 7.

wide range of products and services and the work of the Vodafone Foundation, we believe we can have the greatest influence over the delivery of five of the UN SDGs" (p. 4).

External assurance of information

There is growing awareness that external independent assurance of the information contained in sustainability reports is also vitally important in providing comparability, transparency and credibility regarding support of the SDGs. In making the case for increasing external assurance, KPMG (2011), for example, suggested that "as corporate responsibility reporting begins to play a larger role in the way stakeholders and investors perceive corporate value, companies should increasingly want to demonstrate the quality and reliability of their corporate responsibility data" (p. 28). Assurance, simply defined as a process used to provide confidence as to the degree of reliance that can be placed on the reported data, can be undertaken in a number of ways. However, the most widely used approach to CSR assurance is the commissioning of an assurance statement by an independent external organisation and such an approach would seem to have claims to provide credibility, integrity and reliability to the reporting process on progress against SDG-related targets.

Within the business sectors covered in this book, there is some evidence of independent external assurance in the sustainability reporting process. HSBC, for example, committed itself to providing an annual progress report, which includes both allocation and impact reporting. The allocation report focuses on the aggregate amounts of funds allocated to each of the SDGs and a description of the types of businesses and projects financed, while the impact report provides quantitative details. HSBC also commissioned an external assurance process to review its annual progress reports and reported that both the progress report and the external assurance statement would be available to the public via the Internet. Another example is provided by NH Hotels, who employed KPMG to undertake an "Independent Limited Assurance on Corporate Responsibility Report" to their 2018 report (NH Hotels, 2018, Annex).

The inclusion of a robust and rigorous assurance statement within sustainability reports helps to enhance reliability and credibility of a company's claimed contribution to the SDGs. More commercially, the provision of an assurance statement might be seen to enhance both a company's reputation with its stakeholders and help to promote its brand identity. Without comprehensive independent external assurance, there is the danger, for example, of large companies being accused of what Dentsu Aegis Network (2018) described as "SDG Wash," which has clear parallels with "Greenwash," the environmentally pejorative term used when green communication messages are deceptively used to promote the perception that a company's products, aims or policies are environmentally friendly. Dentsu Aegis Network (2018) argue that SDG Wash damages "the relationship of trust between consumers and individual companies" (p. 13), which underscores the value of robust external assurance.

The key role of information and communications technology

Information and communications technologies are playing a key role in facilitating the SDGs and this role will only get greater as we approach 2030. Matt Granryd, director general of the ICT cross-industry body GSMA, stated, "As an industry we have an important opportunity to leverage the mobile networks that we have built and the services we deliver to help achieve the Sustainable Development Goals" (GSMA, 2016, p. 5). The rapid pace of technological development within the ICT industry may revolutionise how the SDGs can be achieved. Ericsson and the Earth Institute Columbia University (2016) commented, "ICTs have the potential to increase the rate of diffusion of a very wide range of technologies across the economy" and "the accelerated uptake of these technologies . . . constitutes the key to achieving the SDGs by their target date of 2030" (p. 12). GeSI, with particular reference to SDG12, noted the future significance of "smart manufacturing," encompassing the industrial Internet of Things, 3-D printing, data analytics, cloud computing, drones and robotics and embedded system production technologies and of "smart agriculture," including automated irrigation systems, real time weather information, and enhanced traceability and tracking systems. Similarly, in addressing SDG3, Microsoft (2017) reported on its role in aiding governments and health-care providers to "understand how to apply technologies like advanced data analytics and cloud solutions to transform healthcare" (p. 4). As regards the mobile technology, GSMA (2016) identified SDGs 1, 4, 9 and 13 as "the SDG targets that the mobile industry can impact in a significant way" (p. 17) and that can "be materially influenced by what the industry currently does" (p. 19).

There is a range of issues around the deployment of ICTs that are discussed in more detail in Chapter 2: their varying impact in different parts of the world, the barriers and challenges that need to be addressed, and the vital facilitating role of governments. GeSI (2016) observe that financial barriers are most acute within less developed economies, where sustainability challenges are often most pressing, and their report called on "the private sector and policy makers alike to create a financial environment that fosters digital innovations that further sustainable development" (p. 35).

Many of the leading players in the business sectors covered in the earlier chapters have recognised the role and importance of technology in changing the nature of their own industries. Christian Finckh, chief HR officer at Allianz SE, for example, notes, "The transition to the digital economy is irreversible. We are working as one Allianz to turn this development into benefits for our customers and employees" (Allianz, 2017, p. 56). Less evident or explicitly stated, outside of the ICT industry, is the potential impact of new technologies on the delivery of the SDGs by *all* industry sectors. The unprecedented nature and pace of technology development may provide sustainable solutions to seemingly elusive environmental and social challenges, and make a major and lasting contribution to the SDGs. Heeks (2016) has noted that the scope, reach and depth of ICTs in developing countries is changing apace and he foresees the emergence, prior to 2030, of a "new digital development paradigm" (p. 1). If Heeks' vision of the future is correct, it will provide a significantly different technology and business framework within which industry sectors can support the SDGs in both the developed and developing worlds.

Managing the contradictions between economic growth and sustainability

There is a body of literature and a line of thinking that question whether economic growth, dependent on the continuing depletion of the earth's finite natural resources, is compatible with sustainable development. Jackson (2006), for example, maintained that "it is entirely fanciful to suppose that deep emission and resource cuts can be achieved without confronting the structure of market economies" (p. 20). Equally pointedly, Fernando (2003) asserted that "capitalism has shown remarkable creativity and power to undermine the goals of sustainable development" (p. 1). More radically, a number of social scientists offer critiques of the relationship between sustainability and continuing economic growth essentially based in political economy. Mansfield (2009), for example, argued that the mainstream approaches to sustainability fail to recognise "the political nature of the socio-economic processes that produce environmental degradation poverty and injustice – in short the political nature of sustainability" (p. 37). Higgins (2013) concluded "the economic growth we know today is diametrically opposed to the sustainability of our planet" (para.10).

The growing commitments to the circular economy may offer a business solution to sustainable development and to how companies can contribute to the SDGs. Fiat Chrysler Automobiles Group (2018), for example, report that their "sustainability practices help support global efforts to stimulate the transition toward a circular economy that is focused on maximizing the value and use from materials, products and waste" and that "FCA favors a well thought-out and balanced approach that addresses a full spectrum of opportunities" (p. 78). Such a transition to a circular economy, however, will both drive and demand major changes in consumer behaviour and consumption patterns. This could see, for example, the growth of a larger service economy with a greater accent on consumers leasing products, rather than on purchasing and owning products. Retailers would need to reframe their relationships with consumers, which may involve, for example, digitally monitoring the performance of products and enabling customers to repair products easily. Here again, technology will play a key role (Jones & Wynn, 2019). Hewlett-Packard (2017), for example, notes they are "transforming how we design, produce, deliver, and reuse products to drive progress toward a more efficient, circular, and low-carbon economy" (p. 27).

Some authors have cast doubt on the value of the circular economy within corporate capitalism, seeing it as a justification for continuing economic growth. Valenzuela and Böhm (2017) comment that "given the all too obvious social and environmental crises associated with out-of-bounds growth capitalism, the circular economy has been one of the main references for rebuilding and reforming a political economy of sustainable growth" (p. 23). A transition to the circular economy would certainly constitute a dramatic change in the way in which consumers approach consumption, and it seems likely to challenge the social value, which consumers ascribe to many products and services. At its most extreme, this might be seen to be reflected in the view that "we are what we buy" and as such may make it difficult for many consumers to buy into second hand or reusable patterns of consumption. It remains to be seen how enthusiastically consumers will embrace the realities of the circular economy, not least in that it might be seen by many as a reverse of progress towards a better life that involved "a sacrifice of our current, tangible needs and desires, in the name of a better but uncertain future" (European Commission, 2012, p. 9).

While the circular economy has a strong environmental focus, much less attention has been paid to the social dimension. Murray, Skene and Haynes (2015), for example, argued that the circular economy "is virtually silent on the social dimension, concentrating on the redesign of manufacturing and service systems to benefit the biosphere" (p. 22). A number of issues may be important here. While the transition to a circular economy will bring socio-economic benefits – for example, in terms of the creation of new employment opportunities associated with the establishment of recycling facilities – issues may arise in terms of the quality of such opportunities, the reward levels associated with them and the geographical distribution of such benefits at regional, national and international levels. More generally, the impact of an increasingly important circular economy on social and intergenerational equity, seen to be fundamental to the SDGs, may prove to be a complex and testing set of issues.

There are thus, arguably, fundamental issues concerning the tension between the efficacy of looking to contribute to the achievement of the SDGs and business imperatives. These tensions are perhaps most markedly manifest in corporate commitments to growth and thus collectively to continuing economic growth, and the impact of such growth on the levels of natural resource use and the environmental impacts attendant upon such growth. At the same time, it is important to recognise that there may be a variable relationship between economic growth and environmental costs and that such environmental costs are often higher in countries in the early stages of economic growth. This can be problematic in establishing and developing large new business ventures in countries in the early stages of economic development where the issues the SDGs are looking to address are often most pressing. Nevertheless, the overwhelming majority of the companies in the business sectors covered in this book are certainly committed to continuing business growth and this in turn, reflects the overwhelmingly dominant thinking within orthodox economics that growth is good. While some companies do not publicly recognise the tensions between sustainability and economic growth, others publicly view such tensions creatively rather than destructively. Eccles (2018), for example, recently noted,

> The SDGs are about making the world a better place. That is not the primary reason companies exist, although the state of the world matters to them. Thus, they should work to create a better world while still delivering the expected returns to their shareholders.
>
> *(para. 1)*

In conclusion, there is a widespread, though perhaps not a universal, belief that the business community has a vital role to play in contributing to the achievement of the SDGs. In some ways, the corporate business community is to be commended for its public commitment to what is a daunting sustainable development agenda. However, if that contribution is to be made, then all companies will need to address a number of potentially difficult and costly challenges that may threaten their current business models and possibly their very existence. Whether corporate executives and investors are currently genuinely prepared to face up to such challenges remains to be seen. Although the increasing incidence of extreme weather events across the world are often regarded as harbingers of seemingly inevitable climate change, they quickly seem to be largely – though not entirely – forgotten and simply brushed aside. In truth, it may require a truly cataclysmic global event to trigger collective rather than individual self-interest to precipitate widespread corporate engagement with the SDGs. A more optimistic view is that the SDGs have given new impetus to the drive for sustainability and that we are now witnessing a shift "from viewing sustainability as a cost centre to recognizing it as an opportunity to reduce risk, improve relationships with customers and employees, and spur business growth and innovation" (Globe, 2014, p. 1). It is to be hoped that this more positive reading of events prevails in the years up to 2030 and beyond.

References

Allianz. (2017). *Responding to tomorrow's challenges: Allianz group sustainability report 2017.* Retrieved June 4, 2019, from www.allianz.com/content/dam/onemarketing/azcom/Allianz_com/investor-relations/en/results/2017-fy/180410-en-Sustainability-Report-2017.pdf

AXA. (2017). *In real life: 2017 integrated report.* Retrieved June 10, 2019, from https://www-axa-com.cdn.axa-contento-118412.eu/www-axa-com%2F2d414b6f-ac38-44ad-bf1d-0fc4b2a231f2_axa-ra2017-en-pdf-e-accessible_03.pdf

Bali Swain, R. (2018). A critical analysis of the sustainable development goals. In W. Leal Filho (Ed.), *Handbook of sustainability science and research* (pp. 341–356). Cham: Springer.

BNP Paribas. (2019). *Corporate social responsibility.* Retrieved June 4, 2019, from https://group.bnpparibas/en/group/corporate-social-responsibility

BP. (2017). *BP sustainability report 2017 – how will BP respond to global change.* Retrieved November 30, 2018, from www.bp.com/content/dam/bp/en/corporate/pdf/sustainability-report/group-reports/bp-sustainability-report-2017.pdf

Citibank. (2017). *Banking on 2030: Citi and the sustainable development goals.* Retrieved May 25, 2019, from www.citigroup.com/citi/about/citizenship/download/Banking-on-2030-Citi-and-the-SDGs-Report.pdf?ieNocache=165

Crane, A., Palazzo, G., Spence, L. J., & Matten, D. (2014). Contesting the value of creating shared value. *California Management Review, 56*(2), 130–154.

Dell. (2017). *Dell and the United Nation's sustainable development goals.* Retrieved October 16, 2018, from www.businessfor2030.org/dell/

Dentsu Aegis Network. (2018). *SDG communications guide.* Retrieved June 16, 2019, from www.dentsu.com/csr/team_sdgs/pdf/sdgs_communication_guide.pdf

Eccles, R. G. (2018). *The importance of the healthcare sector to the sustainable development goals.* Retrieved June 3, 2019, from www.forbes.com/sites/bobeccles/2018/07/01/the-importance-of-the-healthcare-sector-to-the-sustainable-development-goals/#7ed6b8ae67a3

Eccles, R. G., Krzus, M., Rogers, J., & Serafeim, G. (2012). The need for sector-specific materiality and sustainability reporting standards. *Journal of Applied Corporate Finance, 24*(2), 8–14.

Ericsson and the Earth Institute Columbia University. (2016). *ICT & SDGs: Final report.* Retrieved June 20, 2019, from www.ericsson.com/assets/local/news/2016/05/ict-sdg.pdf

European Commission. (2012). *Policies to encourage sustainable consumption.* Retrieved August 8, 2017, from http://ec.europa.eu/environment/eussd/pdf/report_22082012.pdf

Fernando, J. L. (2003). Rethinking sustainable development. In *The annals of the American academy of political and social science.* London: Sage Publications. Retrieved March 15, 2014, from www.sagepub.com/booksProdDesc.nav?currTree=Subjects&level1=B00&prodId=Book227408

Fiat Chrysler Automobiles Group. (2018). *Sustainability report 2018.* Retrieved June 21, 2019, from www.fcagroup.com/en-US/investors/financial_information_reports/sustainability_reports/sustainability_reports/FCA_2018_Sustainability_Report.pdf

Fujitsu. (2018). *SDG-related activities in Fujitsu.* Retrieved October 16, 2018, from www.fujitsu.com/global/about/csr/vision/sdgs/

Future Earth. (2015). *Review of targets for the sustainable development goals: The science perspective.* Retrieved December 18, 2018, from www.futureearth.org/news/global-sustainable-development-goals-need-clearer-more-measurable-targets-according-new-report

GeSI. (Global e-Sustainability Initiative and Accenture Strategy). (2016). *System transformation: How digital solutions will drive progress towards the sustainable development goals.* Retrieved August 23, 2018, from http://systemtransformation-sdg.gesi.org/160608_GeSI_System Transformation.pdf

Global Reporting Initiative. (2013). *Report or explain: A smart EU policy approach to non-financial information disclosure.* Retrieved December 3, 2013, from www.globalreporting. org/resourcelibrary/GRI-non-paper-Report-or-Explain.pdf

Global Reporting Initiative. (2014). *Materiality: What topics should organizations include in their reports?* Retrieved June 16, 2019, from www.globalreporting.org/SiteCollection Documents/Materiality.pdf

Globe. (2014, March 26–28). *Sustainable consumption and retail – round table: Is sustainable retail an oxymoron?* Thirteenth Biennial Conference and Trade Fair on Business and the Environment. Conference Program. Vancouver, Canada. Retrieved May 15, 2019, from www.globeseries.com/forum2012/conference/conference-program/sustainable-consumption-retail.html

Governance and Accountability Institute. (2014). *Sustainability-what matters.* Retrieved June 16, 2019, from www.ga-institute.com/fileadmin/user_upload/Reports/G_A_ sustainability_-_what_matters_-FULL_REPORT.pdf

GSMA (*Groupe Speciale Mobile* Association). (2016). *2016 mobile industry impact report: Sustainable development goals.* Retrieved January 23, 2017, from www.gsma.com/betterfuture/wp-content/uploads/2016/09/_UN_SDG_Report_FULL_R1_WEB_Singles_LOW.pdf

GSK. (GlaxoSmithKline). (2016). *Our commitment to the sustainable development goals.* Retrieved February 8, 2019, from https://ca.gsk.com/media/1301873/our-commitment-to-sustainable-development-update.pdf

Heeks, R. (2016). Examining digital development: The shape of things to come. *Development informatics.* Working Paper Series, No. 63. Retrieved March 21, 2017, from https:// mecon.nomadit.co.uk/pub/conference_epaper_download.php5?PaperID

Hewlett Packard. (2017). *HP 2017 sustainable impact report.* Retrieved November 8, 2018, from https://h20195.www2.hp.com/V2/getpdf.aspx/c05179523.pdf

Higgins, K. L. (2013). *Economic growth and sustainability- are they mutually exclusive?* Retrieved June 14, 2019, from www.elsevier.com/connect/economic-growth-and-sustainability-arethey-mutually-exclusive

Hyatt. (2018). *Corporate responsibility at Hyatt.* Retrieved June 14, 2019, from https://about. hyatt.com/en/hyatt-thrive.html

IHG. (2018). *Responsible business report 2018.* Retrieved May 24, 2019, from www.ihgplc. com/en/responsible-business

ITV. (2004). *One ITV – corporate responsibility report 2004.* Retrieved June 16, 2019, from https://responsiblemediaforum.org/downloadDocumentFile?document=55

ITV. (2017). *ITV responsibility: Corporate responsibility summary report 2017.* Retrieved June 16, 2019, from http://itvresponsibility.com/resources/itv-corporate-responsibility-report-2017/

Jackson, T. (2006). Readings in sustainable consumption. In T. Jackson (Ed.), *The Earthscan reader in sustainable consumption* (pp. 1–12). London: Earthscan.

John Lewis & Partners. (2018). *Corporate responsibility report 2017–8.* Retrieved May 11, 2019, from www.johnlewispartnership.co.uk/content/dam/cws/pdfs/our-responsibili ties/2018/jlp-cr-report-201718-digital.pdf

Johnson & Johnson. (2019). *Our SDG commitment.* Retrieved February 13, 2019, from www. jnj.com/sustainable-development-goals

Jones, P., & Wynn, M. (2019). The circular economy, natural capital and resilience in tourism and hospitality. *International Journal of Contemporary Hospitality Management, (31)*6, 2544–2563. ISSN 0959-6119. https://doi.org/10.1108/IJCHM-05-2018-0370

KPMG. (2011). *KPMG international survey of corporate responsibility reporting.* Retrieved November 11, 2014, from www.kpmg.com/Global/en/IssuesAndInsights/Articles Publications/corporate-responsibility/Documents/2011-survey.pdf

KPMG. (2018). *How to report on the SDGs.* Retrieved May 31, 2019, from www.iau-hesd. net/sites/default/files/documents/how-to-report-on-sdgs.pdf

Kroger. (2018). *Kroger sustainability report 2018: Setting the table for a sustainable future.* Retrieved May 12, 2019, from http://sustainability.kroger.com/Kroger_CSR2018.pdf

Liverman, D. (2018). Geographical perspectives on development goals: Constructive engagement and critical perspectives on the MDs ad the SDGs. *Dialogues in Human Geography, 8*(2), 168–185.

Mansfield, B. (2009). Sustainability. In N. Castree, D. Demeriff, D. Liverman, & B. Rhoads (Eds.), *A companion to environmental geography* (pp. 37–49). London: Wiley.

Melia Hotels International. (2016). *Integration of sustainable development goals into Melia International.* Retrieved May 20, 2019, from www.meliahotelsinternational. com/en/press-room/11142016/integration-sustainable-development-goals-sdg-melia-hotels-international

Microsoft. (2017). *Microsoft and the UN sustainable development goals.* Retrieved May 23, 2018, from download.microsoft.com/ . . . /Microsoft%20and%20the%20UN%20SDGs%20 Sept%20 . . .

Mitsubishi. (2018). *CSR materiality and SDGs management.* Retrieved October 16, 2018, from www.mitsubishielectric.com/en/sustainability/csr/management/management/materiality_sdgs/index.html

Moseley, W. G. (2018). Geography and engagement with UN development goals: Rethinking development or perpetuating the status quo. *Dialogues in Human Geography, 8*(2), 201–206.

MSD. (2018). *Corporate responsibility report 2017/8 – sustainable development goals (SDGs) – MSD responsibility.* Retrieved February 2, 2019, www.msdresponsibility.com/our-approach/reporting-frameworks/sustainable-development-goals/

Murray, E., Skene, K., & Haynes, K. (2015). The circular economy: An interdisciplinary exploration of the concept and application in a global context. *Journal of Business Ethics.* [online]. doi:10.1007/s10551-015-2693-2

Nestle. (2017a). *Our approach: Creating shared value.* Retrieved June 16, 2019, from www. nestle.com/csv/what-is-csv

Nestle. (2017b). *Contributing to the global goals.* Retrieved June 16, 2019, from www.nestle. com/csv/what-is-csv/contribution-global-goals

NH Hotels. (2018). *Annual report 2018 – corporate responsibility report.* Retrieved June 8, 2019, from https://memorianh.com/2018/corporate-responsibility-report/

Nissan. (2018). *Sustainability report 2018.* Retrieved October 28, 2018, from www.nissan-global.com/EN/SUSTAINABILITY/REPORT/

OECD. (2017). *Getting governments organised to deliver on the sustainable development goals.* Retrieved June 20, 2019, from www.oecd.org/gov/SDGs-Summary-Report-WEB.pdf

Porter, M. E., & Kramer, M. R. (2011). Creating shared value. *Harvard Business Review, 89*(1), 2–17.

Publicis. (2018). *Sustainable development goals.* Retrieved April 30, 2019, from http://publicis groupe-csr-smart-data.com/en/sdgs/

PWC. (2017). *SDG reporting challenge 2017: Exploring business communication on the global goals.* Retrieved June 16, 2019, from www.pwc.com/gx/en/sustainability/SDG/pwc-sdg-reporting-challenge-2017-final.pdf

PWC. (2018). *SDG reporting challenge: SDG prioritisation – is business on the right track?* Retrieved June 16, 2019, from https://pwc.blogs.com/sustainability/2018/01/sdg-prioritisation-is-business-on-the-right-track.html

Shell. (2017). *Sustainability report 2017.* Retrieved December 6, 2018, from http://reports.shell.com/sustainability-report/2017/our-contribution-to-society/sustainable-development-goals.html

Society of Motor Manufacturers and Traders (2018). *2018 Automotive sustainability report.* 19th Edition. Retrieved November 7, 2018, from https://www.smmt.co.uk/wp-content/uploads/sites/2/SMMT-Sustainability-Report-2018-1.pdf

Standard Chartered Bank. (2019). *Sustainability aspirations 2019.* Retrieved March 26, 2019, from https://av.sc.com/corp-en/content/docs/sustainability-aspirations-2019.pdf

Toshiba. (2018). *Supporting the United Nations.* Retrieved November 11, 2018, from www.toshibatec.eu/campaigns/un-sustainable-development-goals/

United Nations Department of Economic and Social Affairs. (2015). *International Decade for Action 'WATER FOR LIFE' 2005-2015.* Retrieved October 9, 2019, from https://www.un.org/waterforlifedecade/waterandsustainabledevelopment2015/stakeholders_governments_and_local_authorities.shtml

United Nations Division for Sustainable Development Goals. (2018). *Helping governments and stakeholders make the SGDs a reality.* Retrieved June 16, 2019, from https://sustainabledevelopment.un.org/

United Nations Framework Convention on Climate Change. (2018). *Achieving the sustainable development goal through climate action.* Retrieved June 15, 2019, from https://unfccc.int/achieving-the-sustainable-development-goals-through-climate-action

Valenzuela, F., & Böhm, S. (2017). Against wasted politics: A critique of the circular economy. *Ephemera: Theory and Politics in Organisation, 17*(1), 23–60.

Vodafone. (2018). *Our contribution to the UN SDGs.* Vodafone. Retrieved November 14, 2018, from www.vodafone.com/content/dam/vodafone-images/sustainability/downloads/sdgs.pdf

Volvo Group. (2017). *Annual and sustainability report 2017.* Retrieved October 29, 2018, from www.volvogroup.com/content/dam/volvo/volvo-group/markets/global/en-en/investors/reports-and-presentations/annual-reports/annual-and-sustainability-report-2017.pdf

GLOSSARY OF TERMS

Artificial Intelligence the use computer systems to perform tasks normally requiring human intelligence, such as visual perception, speech recognition or decision-making.

Assurance a process used to provide confidence as to the degree of reliance that can be placed on reported data, notably in the case of sustainability reporting and alignment with the SDGs. This may involve the commissioning of an assurance statement by an independent external organisation (External Assurance).

Big Data the use of large amounts of data usually obtained from external sources to support company reporting and analysis.

Cloud Computing accessing your systems and data located externally, "in the cloud," via the Internet.

Corporate Governance comprises a combination of processes, rules and activities that underpin the direction and control of a company. It balances the interests of a company's many stakeholders and often now encompasses corporate sustainability.

Corporate Social Responsibility (CSR) an organisation's set of processes and activities that ensures social accountability – to itself, its stakeholders and the public. By practising CSR, companies can be conscious of the kind of impact they are having on all aspects of society including economic, social and environmental areas. A CSR report will now often include sections on sustainability and the SDGs.

Internet of Things the use of devices and monitors linked to the Internet to record data, which can then be stored in your main business systems and databases.

Key Performance Indicators (KPIs) quantifiable measures used to assess the success or otherwise of an organisation or individual in meeting objectives for performance.

Materiality   the concept of materiality (or material issues) can be traced to the auditing and accounting processes associated with traditional financial reporting, but it is increasingly seen to be vitally important in sustainability reporting. Materiality is essentially concerned with whether the issues, impacts and concerns in the CSR report are relevant and important to stakeholders looking to make informed judgements about the extent to which a company is discharging its social responsibilities.

Paris Climate Agreement   a landmark agreement to combat climate change and set in place actions and commitments necessary for a sustainable, low-carbon future. The Paris Agreement aims to keep global temperature rise this century well below 2 degrees Celsius above pre-industrial levels and to pursue efforts to limit the temperature increase even further to 1.5 degrees Celsius.

SDG Wash   a superficial and non-effective approach to supporting and advancing the SDGs.

Sustainable Bond   a financial product that allows loans to be made to finance projects that bring clear environmental and social-economic benefits. Some of these bonds now directly reference the SDGs.

Sustainable Consumption   central to SDG12 and concerns the measures needed to promote resource and energy efficiency, sustainable infrastructure and provide access to basic services and a better quality of life for all, at a time when material consumption of natural resources is on the increase worldwide.

Sustainable Development   often seen as "development that meets the needs of the present without compromising the ability of future generations to meet their own needs" (World Commission on Environment and Development, 1987, p. 12).

Sustainable Development Goals (SDGs)   came into effect in January 2016 and will guide UN development thinking and policy up to 2030. They consist of 17 goals, 169 targets and 241 indicators.

Reference

World Commission on Environment and Development. (1987). *Our common future*. Retrieved June 9, 2019, from https://sustainabledevelopment.un.org/content/documents/5987our-common-future.pdf

INDEX

Note: Page numbers in *italics* indicate a figure and page numbers in **bold** indicate a table.

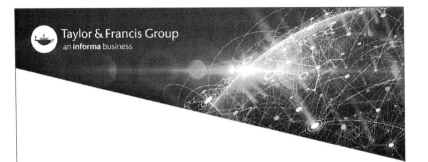